Best wishes,

[signature]

[signature]

HAUNTING CHANTS SILENT STONES

A colourful, and often amusing, story of a couple who, frustrated with the monotony of commuting to London each day, decided to fulfil an ambition. Accepting the inevitable risks of unemployment, they embarked on a three-month tour of Great Britain, visiting the ruined medieval abbeys, cathedrals, and other historic monuments along their route.

Written from a personal diary of the tour, it is a factual account accompanied by many photographs and paintings to tempt the reader to explore further at his leisure.

Wrapper Illustration: Talley Abbey — **Carmarthenshire**
Only surviving section of the crossing tower

HAUNTING CHANTS
SILENT STONES

An evocative tour through medieval Britain

Linda Lee & Laurie Jonas

ARTHUR H. STOCKWELL LTD.

Elms Court   Ilfracombe   Devon

Established 1898

British Library Cataloguing-in-Publication Data.
A catalogue record for this book is available
from the British Library.

ISBN 0 7223 3258-0
Printed in Great Britain by
Arthur H. Stockwell Ltd.
Elms Court   Ilfracombe
Devon

Acknowledgements

Jack & Daphne, Don & Hettie (our folks), for their support and enthusiasm.

Don Jonas for contributing some great paintings and sketches.

Dottie for housesitting while we were 'on the road'.

Viv, for planting 'the seed'.

Chris, who helped make the venture a reality.

The staff of English Heritage, CADW, Historic Scotland, The National Trust and The Church of England and other proprietors who took time to share their knowledge with us.

And a special 'thank you' to Mother Concordia Scott, OSB.

The photograph on the wrapper of the authors
is by courtesy of Ronald White Studios, Maidstone.

Dedicated to those people who, quietly and unnoticed,
spend their daily lives protecting our rich heritage,
from the ravages and greed of the 20th Century.

CONTENTS

GISBOROUGH PRIORY

Pen and watercolour sketch of the remaining east end of Gisborough Priory

Preface

"Passengers waiting on Platform 1 for the 7.06 to Cannon Street are advised that this service has been cancelled. Please wait for further announcements." What will this morning's excuse be for the all too familiar unreliability of our rail service to London. Will it be a major points failure? Maybe signalling problems? Perhaps the mysterious lack of rolling stock (where does it disappear to overnight?), or simply that the crew did not turn up? One thing that is a guaranteed certainty, when a train does eventually arrive, it will be heaving with heavily-clad, sweaty bodies; the carriages will be suffocatingly airless, and there will be standing space only between the assortment of bags, briefcases, books and newspapers! At least there are 'no smoking' zones now so we won't have to suffer the embarrassment of arriving at the office smelling like last night's ashtray!

Meanwhile, we wait patiently on the crowded platform, huddled together for warmth and protection against the raw wind that's trying to cut our legs from beneath us. It's little wonder that we are prone to colds and infections at this time of the year, because after shivering for an inordinate length of time on an exposed, draughty platform, we will suddenly be plunged into a confined and steaming space, resembling a sauna! At times like these, we seriously question why we continue to put up with the unnecessary stress and aggravation for some forty-eight weeks of the year — and pay £2,000 for the so-called privilege?

The answer always appeared to be fairly obvious, until one day. In association with many of our travelling companions, we often used to discuss what else we could do to earn a decent living, but nothing viable ever sprung readily to mind. So the weeks, months and years continued to pass in a blur of rushing, waiting, standing, working, sleeping, and becoming more frustrated and dissatisfied with the quality of life.

Seasoned commuters can identify with the fact that travelling to one's workplace in a major city follows a strictly regimental code; you arrive at the station each morning at precisely the same time; you stand on exactly the same spot on the platform; you enter the same carriage; and you sit (hopefully), in the same seat. Because of these habitual traits, it isn't too long before you strike up an acquaintance with the group of passengers sharing your carriage and, in time, start to exchange the mundane niceties of what you do, what interests and hobbies you have, where you holiday, etc.

With fourteen hours every day taken up with travelling, and working in demanding full-time jobs, we used to alleviate the physical and mental fatigue periodically by arranging long weekend breaks. These became our release valves, as they provided the motivation to get through the weekly agony. With a relatively inexpensive four-day break exploring a particular county or region of the country, this gave us the much-needed tonic to get back onto the treadmill and work towards the next one. Laurie, being the model Project Manager, would ensure that not one moment of these quarterly breaks was 'wasted' with unaccountable periods of time. An area was chosen, the accommodation arranged, and a full itinerary for each day was drawn up, in conjunction with a variety of guidebooks, information leaflets, and a detailed road map. These vital moments spent on planning ensured that we got the most out of our brief forays into previously undiscovered territory. Historical monuments, stately homes, country manor houses, gardens, wildlife parks, and any other features of interest peculiar to the locality would form the basis of the agenda.

Following our 'awaydays' and returning to the daily drudgery of commuting, we would bore our travelling companions with bundles of photographs and associated tales of our latest adventures. They always appeared amazed at the number and diversity, of places we were able to fit in, and commented that, when they took similar breaks, the time had 'simply vanished' before they'd even had a chance to discover any of the local attractions. We assured them that there was nothing difficult in achieving this coverage — all it required was a bit of investigation and research into the area before setting off. At this point, I will admit I always used to prefer the 'ad hoc' approach to taking a break, but am now a firm believer in the essence of planning to get the most out of the limited time available. A good friend, and travelling companion, of ours once mooted "It would be a good idea if there were books or leaflets available suggesting an itinerary for short breaks in specific areas". Giving this scenario time to seep into the old, grey matter, the first germ of an idea was cultivated.

Maybe we could produce some informative guides on areas of the country we had already visited, but where would we start? As amateurs, who could only pursue such avenues on a part-time basis, we thought a more realistic approach might be for us to prepare some short articles, with photographs, and send them to appropriate magazines. However, with no experience in the freelance marketplace, and knowing how competitive it was, we felt it necessary to gain some credibility and recognition before editors would be prepared to accept our work.

Expanding our thought process even further, we came up with the ultimate solution; we could produce a book, which would become our portfolio for future commissions — if it worked! Of course, the foremost important question we had to ask ourselves was could we exchange our IT and Personnel Management skills for those needed to set up a successful partnership as freelance writer and photographer? With a confidence we portrayed to each other (but not one that I'm convinced either of us really felt at the time), we decided to give it our best shot and 'go for the pipedream'.

Two years on from that first, sceptical notion, and the concept has now blossomed from the embryonic stage to one that is about to reach fruition. Facing the dilemma of how to cover such a wealth of heritage, we hit upon the idea of 'themed' tours. We then researched the market to find what type of books were currently available. There appeared to be many publications covering castles, manor houses and gardens but very little written recently on the medieval abbeys, and what did exist were largely heavy-going, factual reference books. As abbeys were a firm favourite of ours, we decided to use the ruined abbey sites as the foundation for the book, but would also include a short reference to other places of interest we visited.

We then felt an 'edge' should be incorporated, for additional interest, and this would be something that many people could relate to. Would the sacrifice of our careers, our adjustment of lifestyle to fulfil this ambition, and the fact that it would be something of a family venture, be the kind of inspiration that would appeal to potential readers?

Laurie could provide the photographs, his dad (a local, amateur artist) could contribute with paintings and sketches, and I could attempt to write the accompanying text. In short, an easy-to-read, lavishly illustrated, 'coffee-table' book.

Laurie drew up the grand project plan, which we worked through in every spare moment of time during the next eighteen months.

THE PLAN

- Research all ruined abbey sites
- Draw up lists of sites to be visited
- Plot suggested routes on map
- Estimate length of trip
- Investigate the most cost-effective method of completing the tour
- Determine the start date of the tour
- Choose and pre-book appropriate accommodation
- Prepare financial breakdown
- Make provisions for a 'home base'

We began by building up a library of historical and ecclesiastical information, with much rummaging through second-hand bookshops. Complimented by our personal knowledge of many abbey sites from previous weekend excursions, we started to identify the sites likely to form the core of the book. The ultimate criteria in making this selection was the inspirational appeal they would have to potential readers. If we could instil sufficient interest to motivate readers to explore one of these evocative places, previously unconsidered by them, then we would be happy that we had achieved our aim. Several weeks later, three definitive lists were compiled: List A, comprising all potential abbey sites (both ruined and complete); List B, cathedrals and castles (for future reference and research purposes); and List C, a miscellany of venues of general interest.

Having plotted all sites using the three 'lists', we proceeded to map out a logical route to ensure efficient coverage of these locations. Several factors were taken into consideration at this stage of the planning, not least two essential visits back home. It is relevant to point out at this stage that Laurie belongs to that unfortunate group of 'part-time' Dads, and has responsibility for his two children on alternate weekends. However, because of the logistics involved during this tour, it would only be possible to return home every fourth weekend. With this firm commitment, as well as other family matters and domestic arrangements, it was decided to plan the tour in three legs which, we estimated, would take about a month each to complete.

Our next decision involved weighing up the pros and cons of various methods of travel and accommodation to be used throughout this period. Would the best idea be to use our car and find B & Bs each night? Would it be more sensible to buy/hire a caravan and tow it to each destination? Or would it be more flexible, and cost-effective, to consider hiring (or even buying) a middle-of-the-range motorhome? After some thorough investigation, and much juggling of figures, we agreed to buy a motorhome. Although this meant a sizeable, capital outlay initially, we were assured that we would make only a negligible loss should we choose to sell it at the end of our tour. Against the outrageous price of hiring the same vehicle for three months, there really was no competition!

Knowing where we were heading for, and how we would get there, we then had to decide on a commencement date for this venture. The significant factor in this process was ease of access to the sites and, as many of them had seasonal opening times, we targeted 2nd April as The Day! (April Fool's Day was avoided for obvious reasons.) Having chosen this time of the year, with the Easter holiday period and a May bank holiday weekend not far off, our next task was to ensure that space was available at the camp sites now identified along our planned route. This particular stage of the planning was quite difficult because, not only did we have to estimate how long we intended to stay at each site, but also we had to take into consideration what facilities were available. There were times when we were likely to need specific conveniences like a launderette, shops, or even an electrical hook-up and these instances had to be factored into the overall route plan. Our *Caravan Club Site Directory* looked extremely well-thumbed after four or five days of continual scanning for precisely the right site at the right time — and our telephone bill matched the cost of booking sites for the first three weeks of the trip!

Now we had come this far, in theory, we felt it an appropriate time to work out the financial consequences of such a wonderful plan. For all intents and purposes, we would be unemployed for a minimum of three months, so our first major consideration was putting enough money aside to cover our normal monthly outgoings. This included the mortgage repayments, car and motorhome loans, utilities bills, child maintenance payments, etc. — a hefty sum when totalled as a three-month figure! We then had to find a deposit for the motorhome (plus money to equip the vehicle, and ourselves), estimate running costs, and allow sufficient funds for entry fees, food supplies and any 'unexpected' expenses we may incur during that period. Arriving at the horrifying figure of some £12,000 as a minimum requirement to accomplish this project, we nearly had second thoughts about the whole idea. However, with everything else pointing to perfect timing, we decided it was a 'now or never' situation — we would find the money somehow!

Laurie was also preoccupied with thoughts on how best to approach the problem of developing his film during the trip. As we would be some distance from home, it would be a distinct advantage to be able to develop the films whilst still in the vicinity of the locations where the shots were taken. However, the difficulty facing us here was that with being continually 'on the move', and often out in the middle of nowhere, a developer might not be that easy to locate. Eventually we came to the conclusion that a better method of dealing with the problem would be for Laurie to post off the films to his father every other day. Dad could then use a local shop to process the films on a 24-hour basis and report back to us, via the mobile phone, should we need to revisit a specific site to take another set of photographs. Although Laurie felt this was not an ideal solution, he conceded that it was better than waiting until we returned home at the end of each monthly stage of the tour.

The final stage of the planning almost fell into place by itself. Our concern at being away from home for long periods of time, and not being able to deal with the post, meter readers, gardening, etc., was easily resolved. A good friend of ours was looking for temporary accommodation that spring, and she was delighted to 'housesit' for us in return for providing a communications base. This would be an excellent two-way arrangement.

It was mid-January 1998 and there was one outstanding issue to deal with. The time had come for us to have the courage of our convictions to a degree where we were prepared to give up our permanent jobs and forego all the security they afforded us. Naturally, the financial implications of 'unemployment' were concerning, but (if my rusty book-keeping efforts were to be believed) it appeared to be just about viable. Our 'safety valve', and one we were heavily reliant upon, was the overwhelming demand for IT people generated by the advent of Year 2000. Having gained many years' experience in the IT industry, and only recently completing a not inconsiderable Year

2000 project for an international organisation, Laurie was confident he would be able to negotiate a lucrative contract on his return to the business world.

And so, the deed was done. During the last few weeks of our employment, it was a constant race against time to ensure that everything was in place for the project commencement date of 2nd April. The list of 'things to buy for the trip' seemed endless, and the other list of 'things to organise' was even more daunting. Purchasing our motorhome was certainly an enlightening experience, with a possible 500 different models to choose from. There were high-tops, coach-builts, A-Class, with every engine size, fuel type and manufacturer imaginable — a complete minefield for the uninitiated! Eventually, we opted for a one-year-old, coach-built vehicle which, hopefully, would provide us with the comfort and reliability we were looking for during our tour. We aimed to minimise all possible risks of mechanical/operational failure, which could prevent us from completing the project within the limited timescale.

Next, we had to kit out our new mobile home with all the essential kitchen paraphernalia (of the lightweight, unbreakable type), as well as buying plenty of warm, weatherproof clothing, and several pairs of joggers and sweatshirts (as being able to wash and dry clothes would be a rare luxury).

Inevitably, there were still a number of camera accessories to be bought — just to ensure the range of equipment was comprehensive enough to meet all photographic demands — and 100 rolls of slide film.

Our purchases made, our personal arrangements finalised, and our financial house in order, we now awaited the day of reckoning.

With the fond farewells and good wishes of our work colleagues still ringing in our ears, we made a swift transition from our well-ordered and routine lifestyle to go roaming at will among several centuries of ancient stones in an attempt to seek our destiny.

Through a grey, damp and misty dawn
The eerie shapes of ancient stones appear;

Close your eyes and see the past reborn
And listen for the strains of life once here.

Chapter One

Bob Marley 'Legends' is pulsing in the background, the fresh mussels in white wine and garlic sauce are simmering on the stove — the first of many 'lay-by lunches' we would enjoy on this trip — and the highway to adventure is straight ahead, courtesy of the A1 North.

As we began our simulated Romany lifestyle in the newly-purchased motorhome, my head is whirling with a hundred and one unanswered questions. Would the money last? Would we remain fit and healthy? Would the house be ok? Would we be able to successfully capture and document our experience? Would we get on with each other for twenty-four hours a day in a 20ft x 7ft box on wheels? And so on. However, it's too late now for any second thoughts. The meticulous planning and scheduling had been completed by the Project Manager (turned amateur photographer), and the project start date is 2nd April — today! I suppose the only option is to adopt a more confident and positive attitude, settle the stomach with lunch, and raise a small toast to 'fulfilling the pipedream'.

Almost in sight of our first destination, and I am feeling a little more relaxed. The disorientation, nervous excitement and sheer bloody fright of the unknown territory we are about to experience, are beginning to subside. In fact, I feel quite exhilarated, and certainly committed to enjoying this adventure — having suffered many restless nights churning over all the different scenarios in my subconsciousness, I realise this is a 'one-off' opportunity which must be used to its best advantage. Laurie was also feeling quite apprehensive about visiting our early sites, as they were both new and challenging from a photographic viewpoint. Being of a very confident and self-assured nature usually, these alien feelings of anxiety and nervousness were making him question his ability to produce the outstanding photographs he had promised for inclusion in this book. What was he worrying about? He had seemingly spent a small fortune on all the necessary camera equipment, taken hundreds of 'test' pictures, and read volumes about his chosen subject. He'd even managed to include 'photo-babble' in everyday conversations, using phrases such as 'aperture and speed', 'light refraction', 'diffuser filters', 'over or under expose half a stop'. Whatever it means, all he has to do now is put the theory into practice. No sweat, I say!

However, amidst all this bravado, we were slowly beginning to realise the enormity of our 'readjustment period'. No longer were we reliant upon a guaranteed, regular income to provide a comfortable lifestyle. The time had come for us to believe in ourselves, and hope that what we could achieve in the next three months might give us the opportunity to make a permanent career change, without becoming financially challenged.

Desperately trying to assume our 'work mode', we pulled off the road to follow the sign to Roche Abbey in Yorkshire, to get our first view of one of the many ruined abbeys we hoped to discover on this tour. Having parked the motorhome (affectionately known as the 'Swift') at the top of a narrow lane, and duly kitted out in our 'wets', we took a damp and dismal trek downhill to view the dark, glistening, almost uninviting, remains of this 12th Century Cistercian abbey. The abbey site, divided by The Maltby Beck, is in a quiet, delightfully picturesque setting at the bottom of a deep valley. Although only a medium-sized house, compared to other great Cistercian abbeys in the north of England, the ruins are one of the finest examples of early Gothic architecture in this part of the country. Incidentally, this was one of Capability Brown's first 'gothick' landscape projects and, like so many other 'romantic ruins' of that era, suffered much destruction of the inner court buildings and the cloisters to accommodate his reorganisation and flair. There are only the transepts of the original church still standing to any height, but a reasonably accurate idea of the layout can be formed from the foundations remaining. Laurie was quite pleased to be able to gain some height via a footpath along the rock face of the valley, in order to take a couple of 'snaps' of the overall layout of the site.

Despite the weather, we felt a certain adrenaline rush as we scrambled along the wooded path, where we were met with the deep purple hue of some early bluebells, a delightful show of delicate wood violets peeping shyly from beneath the dripping undergrowth, and a few straggly remnants of the golden, spring daffodils. This was it. Back to nature, freedom, and fresh air. We were doing 'our thing' for real!

On a sunny day, with a background of wild flowers, the birds singing, and the stream gently murmuring along, it would be a perfect spot for a picnic and a few hours' relaxation. Today, however, with heavy skies, persistent rain and a cold wind blowing, it took on an entirely different aspect! Our first night as ex-City gypsies proved to be just about as exciting as one could wish for! Looking forward to reaching our camp site, parking up and enjoying an early dinner with, of course, a good bottle of red wine, seemed an eminently reasonable idea to relieve the tensions of the day. What we didn't bargain on was getting firmly bogged down in a rain-sodden muddy field, which further escalated into two hours of continuous towing attempts, some fairly frayed tempers and plenty of bemused onlookers, before we were again on 'terra firma'. We decided that we'd put that one down to experience.

At last it was time to retire to our cosy little 'snug' above the driving cab — all 6ft x 4ft 6in x 2ft high of it! Great, I thought as the wind roared and rocked the 'Swift', the rain bounced heavily on the fibreglass roof just twenty-four inches above us, and the thunderstorm raged relentlessly overhead. Whatever possessed us to leave our centrally heated, well-insulated house and sit in the middle of a field on such a filthy night encased in a flimsy cocoon? We had to seriously question our sanity — and, maybe, take heed of this bad weather warning!

Having survived an extremely interesting twenty-four hours, we awoke early to a distinct 'freshness' in the air. Negotiating the ladder from the 'snug', Laurie quickly lit the gas fire, put on several layers of clothing and made a cup of tea to warm us through. We sat looking at each other for a while, looked at the weather outside, looked at our route on the map and decided we ought to take full advantage of the fact that is was only 5.30 a.m., and drive on to our next destination.

Rattling along the dual carriageway, it soon became apparent that we were travelling 'up country', as evidenced by that great, rusting monstrosity rising above the horizon — The Angel of the North. What on earth possessed a local council to erect such a huge, gaudy, lump of metal that, for all intents and purposes, looked like the forlorn, dismembered wings of an old war plane — and call it an "Angel"! The passing tourists must surely gaze at this unusual 'landmark' in absolute bewilderment and, as in my own case, sheer disbelief. It is incredible what constitutes modern art. Off the main drag now, and we were driving along the narrow, twisting roads through the rugged Cheviot Hills, with their peaty-coloured streams swelled by the heavy rainfall racing down the barren slopes on either side of us. Just then, through the pale sun's intermittent rays, we caught our first glimpse of the Scottish Border's bracken hills. A little further on and we arrived in the busy town of Melrose, and duly followed the signs leading us to the abbey.

Hoping that the ruins of this Cistercian abbey would more than compensate for the tediously long drive we'd just made through heavy showers and strong winds, we parked our motorhome, donned our waterproof gear, and got the camera equipment ready. Before venturing out to discover this monastic site, however, we decided to seek some internal 'central heating' which a quaint coffee shop provided in the form of piping hot, home-made soup and fresh crusty rolls. Grateful for this 'nice warm feeling' inside, and pleased to see the weather was actually brightening up, we now made our way across to the abbey.

We were not disappointed — the impressive church built of beautiful dusky-pink sandstone stood almost complete, apart from its roof, and there was such ornate detail on the columns, gables and everywhere to be seen — it was really beautiful. With its surviving eight aisle chapels, the magnificent east end perpendicular window tracery, the elegant south transept gable and such an intricate pattern of ribs and bosses on the vaulted ceiling of the presbytery, there is almost too much to take in at first sight.

This has been a religious site for over 800 years. The original 12th Century church was mostly destroyed in the late 14th Century, and was subsequently enlarged in the rebuilding, and this is what remains to be seen today. The site is split by a road running through the middle of the Lay Brothers' Range, on the other side of which, situated beside the mill lade is the Commendator's House. This building is now in use as a museum displaying some of the excavated artefacts from the abbey.

Melrose, a daughter house of Rievaulx, was founded by King David, as was Jedburgh and Kelso and became one of Scotland's wealthiest medieval monasteries, which is still evident from today's magnificent remains.

With a last, lingering look at Melrose we jumped back into the 'Swift', managing to avoid another downpour and, with a quick reference to the map, found our overnight stop at Kelso. We became a bit concerned as we checked into the camp site, as all the pitches were slightly sloping, and on grass. Carefully choosing the most appropriate pitch for this troublesome three-and-a-half ton, we nervously parked up for the night. For the second night in succession, the heavens decided to open on us and, by morning, it was patently obvious that we were going nowhere without some assistance. What a difference a tractor, a tow rope and a friendly site manager can make when you have places to go and sights to see!

On our itinerary today, we had Jedburgh Abbey to visit in the morning and Dryburgh Abbey after lunch. A short drive along the A698 and we were on our way. Even before we arrived in the town, we couldn't fail to notice the impressive dimensions of the abbey as it sat proudly atop the small Scottish community. Finding the main car park, immediately adjacent to the abbey, we parked the 'Swift', prepared lunch, and popped it in the oven to cook slowly. Laurie methodically gathered his photographic gear together, and then we set off to explore this huge Augustinian abbey dominating the town from its high position on the bank of the Jed Water.

Jedburgh, originally founded as a priory in the early 12th Century, was very much a working abbey and although silenced for many years, it retained a strange, busy air within its walls. It was incredible to find such substantial remains of these Border abbeys considering their turbulent history (not to mention several confrontations with the English armies throughout their lifetime). The site slopes steeply down to the river bank and many of the domestic buildings are set on terraced platforms. From a first-floor viewing point, where we could look down the length of the nave, it was easy to visualise the sheer enormity of this wonderful church, which remained in use as the parish church until 1875. Sadly though, and in contrast to Melrose, very little intricate detail remains visible among Jedburgh's ruins. However, in 1986 the lovely cloister garden was reconstructed along the lines of a

Roche Abbey — *South Yorkshire*
*On a dismal day, the surviving transepts present a stark
and eerie reminder of monastic life in the 12th Century*

Melrose Abbey — *Border*
The beautiful abbey church as seen from southwest corner of graveyard

typical 16th Century Scottish monastery garden with its medicinal and pot herbs and plants. As the sun decided to grace us with its presence, albeit for a short burst, I took the opportunity to sit and meditate while Laurie continued to reel off yet another roll of film! This is more of what I expected on the trip — sun, solitude and superb monastic sites.

Whilst in the centre of town, we had to make an essential purchase — two pairs of sturdy, quilted wellies-cum-snow boots to keep our feet warm and dry in the dreadful weather conditions we were experiencing. Rain again determined our departure from Jedburgh, so we hastily consumed the roast dinner prepared earlier in the car park, before proceeding back 'up country' to find Dryburgh Abbey. In its secluded and tranquil setting, surrounded on three sides by the River Tweed, it was in complete contrast to Jedburgh's busy, town environment. The white canons of the Premonstratensian Order, who lived here over 850 years ago, were content to quietly contemplate and prepare themselves for their next life, and this location provided the perfect refuge.

Between trying to dodge the frequent cloudbursts - and a Scottish wedding party trailing in the wake of a professional photographer who, it seemed, wanted to be wherever we were — we walked briskly across the three levels of this terraced site, discovering much ornate carving on the glorious, pink sandstone ruins. The chapterhouse, with its barrel vaulted ceiling, remains virtually in tact as do two of the chapels in the North Transept where, incidentally, the tombs of Sir Walter Scott and Earl Haig can be found.

During the late 18th Century, Dryburgh was purchased by the eleventh Earl of Buchan who took great delight in transforming the old monastic site into a truly romantic ruin, which can still be enjoyed today. When the vast array of wild spring flowers burst into colour, they give a renewed vitality to the huge, ancient boulders that have stood resiliently over many centuries. The aura of serenity here obviously touched 'something' within me because I now felt all the apprehension and tension of the last few days really ease away, to be replaced with a true spirit of adventure, and surprising confidence that 'the mission would be successfully accomplished'.

With the camp site situated just outside of Kelso, we simply had to visit the ruins of Kelso Abbey, originally the largest, and most important, of this group of Border abbeys. This monastery was founded and run by the Tironensian monks, an order which was found nowhere else in the UK. Unusually, the abbey had two crossings — thought to be built from a German design — not unlike Ely Cathedral. There was little evidence of the severity of the Norman architecture among Kelso's fragmented remains, and it was difficult to imagine how proud and wealthy this abbey must have been in the early 13th Century.

Melrose Abbey — **Border**
A stone shield carved with Abbot Hunter's coat of arms

Jedburgh Abbey — **Border**
*Standing in the northwest corner of graveyard to view
the immense remains of this Augustinian abbey*

On reaching our base that evening, we decided to 'play safe' and park up on the gravel path beside the allotted pitch just to give us more than an even chance of pulling away next morning under our own steam. The down side to this, however, was trying to eat dinner off the table rather than off our laps, due to the fairly steep incline of the road, and sleeping with the constant sensation of 'rolling over the edge'. There was also the consideration of whether the fridge would work properly, as the unit was supposed to remain level — not that this would be a significant problem with the current temperatures we were experiencing. Oh well, it's all in a day's work, as they say.

Yet another early-morning drenching for Laurie during his daily maintenance routine of the vehicle; disconnecting the electrical supply and reeling in the cable, turning off the gas supply, taking twenty litres of fresh water on board, and emptying the waste tanks. Initially, the plan was to share these duties but, as he seemed more than willing to ensure everything was shipshape, why volunteer to get thoroughly wet and cold when there's the washing-up, clearing away, sweeping through, etc. to keep me busy inside the vehicle!

Day four and we were heading back across the border into England to see the one place that has been a source of fascination for me since childhood — Lindisfarne. Although our first sighting of Holy Island was through a dense, damp mist, and with a high tide making the causeway impassable, our enthusiasm remained undeterred. Time to park up the 'Swift', put the kettle on, light the fire, read the paper and relax for a while until the tide recedes. Being able to do this was the real benefit of travelling around in a motorhome, and one we would appreciate on several other occasions during the course of the trip.

The queue of cars slowly creeping forward signalled that the water had subsided sufficiently for us to gain access to the island. It was all very exciting driving through the parting waters, and mounds of compact wet sand, as we continued with our journey to Lindisfarne Priory. Arriving at the main visitor centre, we first walked around an extremely informative and well-planned exhibition about the history of Lindisfarne and an insight into the lives of its inhabitants from as early as AD635. Trying to delay the inevitable moment when I knew we would have to brave the elements once more, I browsed among the souvenirs in the English Heritage shop. Laurie 'persuaded' me to purchase a teddy bear (appropriately dressed as a monk) to add to my collection of 'bears-in-a-basket', who were keeping each other company at home beside the fireplace. So with 'Cuthbert' tucked safely under my arm, the essential guidebook and china thimble (something else I like to collect from places we visit), it was now time to venture forth into this desolate, and seemingly inhospitable, site.

Jedburgh Abbey — **Border**
Detail of surviving nave arcade columns

Lindisfarne Priory — **Northumberland**
Some detail remains on these robust Norman columns

Being one of the most important learning centres of Anglo-Saxon England, Lindisfarne became something of a cult centre in the North. The 12th Century priory was one of a number of 'satellite' monasteries controlled by the mother-house at Durham, and monks from Durham were moved around the large network of cells at the prior's discretion. Wandering across the harsh and barren environment today, it was difficult trying to imagine how the monks survived on their diet of very little food and water, especially during bitterly cold winters. Undoubtedly they thought they had arrived at the edge of the world, as written evidence of that time records, and standing here on this chilly, dismal day, I can fully understand their feeling of eerie remoteness from all other civilisation. The ruinous church that is seen today was built on the site of the original, smaller 7th Century church which contained the shrine of St Cuthbert, and many miracles were reported to have taken place here. There are many highly decorative features remaining, and some beautiful arcade columns in the nave. We clambered up onto the headland, beyond the priory walls, to get a better overview of the site. Looking along the coast, we could just make out the shape of Bamburgh Castle perched on a grassy outcrop and facing the sea.

It was very thought-provoking knowing we had just walked through some thirteen hundred years of religious beliefs, teachings and miracles. Quite a mystical and special experience.

Deeply immersed in history and religion, I hadn't realised that some two hours had passed, but my stomach began to drop a few subtle hints that it was about time to refuel! Luckily, there was a convenient pub directly opposite the priory which provided us with a decent Sunday lunch. What a strange contrast; here we were sitting in a comfortable, warm place being well fed whilst, not two hundred yards away (and only five centuries ago!), those dedicated monks were enduring a stark existence at this wild, coastal site.

If tide tables had allowed, we had intended to visit the small castle on the island, but time was against us today and this would have to wait for another occasion. Northumberland has more castles than any other English county, and we had already come to the conclusion whilst planning this trip that our research of these sites would have to form the basis of an independent venture. Leaving Holy Island behind us, and with the faintest glimmer of sunshine breaking through the dark clouds, we take a pleasant drive down the northeast coast to Tynemouth, where we find the remains of a Benedictine priory fortified within the walls of a late medieval castle.

Precariously standing on the edge of an eroding cliff face, looking across the River Tyne, Tynemouth Priory must have endured a constant battering over the years, not only from the prevailing weather conditions but also from 'foreign' invaders. In fact, history suggests that it has been used as the town's

Dryburgh Abbey — **Border**
Remains of abbey almost buried in the spring foliage

Lindisfarne — **Northumberland**
*A murky, North Sea coastal view from the priory grounds
with Bamburgh Castle just visible on the distant horizon*

coastal defence since Roman times. The monastery was colonized by a group of monks, sent by the Prior of St Albans, in the latter part of the 11th Century. Following the Dissolution, King Henry VIII kept Tynemouth as a royal castle and a fortress, and the nave of the church served as the parish church until the 17th Century. Although not too much evidence exists of this once wealthy priory, it is an interesting and unusual site with a very chequered history.

Satisfied that we had completed today's schedule successfully, despite the inclement weather, we were now ready to search out our overnight camp site, somewhere in Whitley Bay. We found the Caravan Club site easily: a beautiful spot on a cliff overlooking the beach, presenting us with good views of the foamy, white waves crashing into the rugged, northerly bay. Feeling quite weary with all this fresh air and change of routine, we were relieved to learn that we wouldn't have any undue aggravation with parking the van as the pitches were all hardstanding. However, what the site manager omitted to tell us was that to get to the pitch we had to drive across a large area of long, thick, spongy grass! We knew from that moment what the implications of this would mean come tomorrow morning and Laurie, being the brilliant Project Manager he is, immediately built in an extra hour to our schedule to accommodate minor inconveniences!

As predicted last night, having breakfasted, showered and got the 'Swift' in operational mode for the day, Laurie then had to seek the help of the Site Manager, and his trusty tractor, to pull us off the pitch. This was becoming a little tiresome so early into the trip — and, to be honest, not something we had even thought about. We just hoped the weather might improve soon to enable us to get off a camp site under our own steam on a more regular basis.

Today we would be endeavouring to undertake the first of our research trips at one of the many cathedrals which we would be passing en route. We found that visiting these sites required a lot more planning and effort for various reasons; neither of us hold a great love for large, bustling cities, so the initial motivation and enthusiasm is somewhat lacking; finding a suitable car park (without height restriction barriers) for the motorhome is often extremely difficult, especially one close enough to enable Laurie to haul along all the necessary photographic equipment required; trying to avoid the services and the 'peak' tourist times; ensuring that photography permits are available without undue bureaucracy and so on.

Notwithstanding all these minor hurdles, we thoroughly enjoy the physical exploration of these magnificent, ancient buildings, the majority of which were monastic abbey churches prior to the Dissolution. It gives an interesting perspective to see the scale and grandeur of the former medieval abbeys in use as cathedrals in busy, city centre environments, when compared to the evocative, romantic ruins left standing in their wild and remote locations.

Having parked quite easily in an excellent car park that actually had various length bays to facilitate vehicles of all shapes and sizes, we carried out our routine procedures of collecting all required gear, donning 'wet' trousers, coats, gloves and wellie boots, before commencing our 'well-laden donkey' impression up the steep hill into the city of Durham. Inside the cathedral we encountered our first major hiccup: a prominent notice displaying 'No photography allowed'. This, in fact, appeared not to be the case, as evidenced by a few people actively taking photographs down the length of the nave. We approached the information desk for clarification, and were duly informed that a photography permit could be issued by the dean, if we cared to part with £10 and walk to the Chapter Steward's offices to purchase a signed permit!

Half an hour later, we re-entered Durham Cathedral and Laurie began his task of gathering a selection of library photographs in the dimly-lit conditions of this vast church. With his efforts completed as best as the lighting would allow, we ventured back outside. Fortunately, the rain had eased considerably, and this encouraged him to wander along the river bank to take some scenic shots, while I made the dreaded trip to the supermarket to stock up on our essential supplies for the coming week. When I rejoined him at our pre-arranged rendezvous, I was met with an extremely wet, muddy and bedraggled version of the man I had left only thirty minutes earlier. Apparently, he'd had a slippery encounter with the river bank whilst scrabbling along it to try for that 'one really good shot'. I am sure it was worth it!

A few miles outside of Durham, we drove on to find Finchale Priory. When we had first researched this site, the historical information available had helped us to form a romantic image of this ruinous priory somewhere 'off the beaten track'. In reality, however, that vision was severely shattered, as we approached the site via a modern automatic barrier with a busy working farm to our right, and a commercial caravan park set beyond the ruins. After our initial disappointment that this wasn't going to conform to the idyllic, dreamy location we had envisaged, we set out to explore the priory in greater detail.

Although relatively small as monastic houses go — accommodating never more than fifteen monks, even in its heyday — it has a fascinating history from its lowly beginnings as a hermitage for St Godric (until his death at the age of 105), to its unusual function as a 'holiday home' in the late 14th Century for the monks of Durham. Had he realised during his severe and lonely lifestyle, that some three hundred years after his death, his meagre home would become a 'Butlins' site for monks, I am sure St Godric would be turning in his grave — which, incidentally is sited behind the choir area. A wonderful view of the entire ruins can be had from the opposite bank of the River Wear, where we enjoyed a fleeting moment of spring sunshine sitting on a bench contentedly licking ice lollies!

Tynemouth Priory — *Tyne & Wear*
The priory ruins seen from the castle gatehouse window

Durham Cathedral — *Co Durham*
*The nave arcade with its vast sculptured columns
showing some similarity to those seen at Lindisfarne*

Watercolour of a beautiful foliated capital at Finchale Priory

We chose our overnight stopping place with two major considerations: firstly, the pitches were all hardstanding and, secondly, it was close to the main A1(M) — for a guaranteed quick getaway in the morning! After all, we were treating ourselves to a 'rest day' with a visit to the Beamish Open Air Museum, and didn't want to risk any unnecessary aggravation to spoil our day of leisure.

By three in the afternoon, we had decided to make tracks towards our next destination as it would be a fairly long drive, and we wanted to settle in at the camp site before the weather changed for the worse again. We felt a strangely comfortable sensation, like that of stepping into old, well-worn slippers, as we were now returning to the familiar landscape of one of our favourite counties. Yorkshire has such a wealth of historical monuments, from spectacular manor houses and gardens, to some of the largest ruined abbeys and priories, that we always have something new to look forward to when visiting this vast area of the country. As we had already decided to indulge ourselves in the glorious expanse of hills, dales, moors and coastal regions, we were staying 'camped up' for six nights just outside Northallerton, which would provide us with a central base from which we could explore.

We eventually arrived at the camp site, situated in a valley just outside the village of Osmotherley. With the increasingly tedious problem of parking the 'Swift' on sodden, unstable ground, Laurie negotiated a compromise with the site owner to allow us to park on the edge of his made-up road rather than on a grassy pitch. Luckily, with the current inclement weather, the park was not that busy so he was able to tuck us out of the way at the bottom of a hill. With our newly-acquired parking skills, we confidently levelled the van into position, and happily settled down for the evening. As far as we could see, our only neighbours were a pair of 'hikers' in a dome tent — oh well, no rush for the showers in the morning!

Off to another dismal start — the showers were only lukewarm, the toilet block was absolutely freezing and we got a second soaking walking back to the 'Swift'. When were we going to get the glorious spring weather we'd come to expect over the past couple of years? I do realise April is traditionally a 'sunshine and showers' month, and I really don't mind the odd shower but persistent, heavy rain, hail, gusting winds and no sun, is stretching one's tolerance a bit too far!

Trying desperately not to get too downhearted, we set out to make our second visit to the delightful Carthusian priory at Mount Grace. Approaching the entrance, we encountered a family of hissing and hostile-looking geese who were not going to make our passage through to the shop an easy task. We carefully avoided these fraught and snappy creatures and wondered what we'd done to distress them so much. Maybe the abysmal weather was causing them undue frustration too, but why take it out on us?

Walking through the shop and into the priory grounds, we were met with a riot of colour. There were large clumps of golden daffodils strewn haphazardly across the lawns, neat borders of vivid red and purple bedding plants, a variety of trees proudly displaying their pretty, delicate blossoms, and lots of thick, matted mosses covering large areas of the old stone walls. On our previous visit, we were fortunate to have seen Mount Grace Priory, at its best, in glorious sunshine to enjoy the full impact of the contrasting colours. But even in today's less than kind weather conditions, the tranquillity and beauty of this plain, but sophisticated priory, still stirs the soul sufficiently to want to explore its depths more thoroughly.

From the substantial remains, it is obvious that this once was a very impressive priory with its Great Cloister encircled by twenty-three individual 'cells' where the Carthusian monks, living as virtual hermits, ate, worked, prayed and slept. One of the cells has been reconstructed to show what the accommodation would have comprised in the 14th Century — it actually looked like a comfortable 'two-up two-down' terraced cottage with a small garden, almost luxurious by traditional monastic standards. Today, however, it was proving to be a convenient shelter for the few visitors who had decided, maybe unwisely, to leave the comfort of their centrally-heated homes to brave these most un-springlike conditions in the quest for a bit of history.

A rare and interesting feature of this site are the pitched roof, stone-built spring houses along the ridge above the priory which fed a water tower situated in the centre of the Great Cloister — clean drinking water and good drainage were essential to Carthusian life.

The fragmented remains of the simple church, used mainly as the meeting place for the 'hermit monks' on special feast days, looks hauntingly suspended in time. The only sign of life is at the top of the bell tower where a screeching raven is industriously engaged in nest-building with the plentiful material from the surrounding woods. A poetic example of new life springing from old!

With a tactful reminder to Laurie that we had two more abbeys on our agenda today, he reluctantly put the camera away, and we left the priory grounds in the capable hands of 'Lord and Lady Puddleduck' who were strolling through the undergrowth in a rather stately manner, thoroughly enjoying all this wetness. I'm glad someone was!

Jumping back onto the A19, we soon covered the twenty miles to reach our next port of call — the great Cistercian Byland Abbey. When the church was originally built, towards the end of the 12th Century, it was the largest in Britain. It also boasted exceptionally large cloisters, measuring some 145 square feet. I do apologise at this point if I seem to be harping on about the

Finchale Priory — *Co Durham*
The scattered remains of this priory from the opposite bank of the River Wear

Mount Grace Priory — *North Yorkshire*
A colourful spring vista through openings in the cloister garth wall

weather, but it has now become nothing short of atrocious. Even the massive west front of Byland Abbey, an unmistakable landmark that can usually be seen long before the site is reached, today portrayed no more than a dark and gloomy shadow through the mist.

Although from our visit last year I can recall seeing several areas of well-preserved floor tiles, many detailed columns and arches, and some lovely examples of blind arcading, I am afraid that today's torrential downpour has beaten me into an early retreat, and I squelched back to the motorhome to prepare something hearty for lunch. Laurie chose to remain among the rain-drenched ruins to take 'just a few more shots', accompanied only by a group of darting chaffinches, who were swooping over the lichen-covered stones hoping that the damp conditions would unearth a tasty lunch for them.

Situated just outside the village of Coxwold, Byland Abbey is a bit out of the way but it is well worth making a detour to catch a glimpse of the magnificently coloured stonework, especially if, like us, you are lucky enough to see it in mellow, autumn sunlight.

Eventually, even Laurie conceded defeat, abandoning any further detailed exploration of the site, being unable to keep the driving rain off his camera and lens. Having tramped soggily back to base, he shook off several layers of saturated garments and exchanged them for warm, dry alternatives. We sat in our cosy quarters, with the gas fire on full, and enjoyed a medium hot chilli that I'd cooked for lunch. As we listened to the incessant pounding of hailstones against the 'Swift', we recalled that this was supposed to be a fun experience, inspiring us to put pen to paper. In truth, I think our creative skills, as such, were currently waterlogged and we needed to dive deeply for the grit and determination to produce some worthwhile copy for a good read! What was plan B?

An hour later and still no let up in the weather, but we agreed to complete the planned schedule for today by driving the short distance over to Rievaulx Abbey, a place that had inspired Laurie since childhood. He had seen a photograph of Rievaulx as an impressionable nine-year-old, and was mesmerised by the sheer enormity and magnificence of this place which seemed so far away. Almost thirty years later he finally gets to visit the vision that sparked his imagination, and now feels that this probably was the single, most determining factor for his present fascination with the ruined, medieval abbeys. Not quite the awesome and romantic image of a young man's fancy in today's thundery conditions, but nevertheless this huge, majestic sight looming out of the depths of a wooded valley retains a certain magical quality.

Rievaulx Abbey was the largest and most important monastery in England, and many other abbeys were colonized by the monks from Rievaulx who followed the Cistercian order. From records kept at the suppression in 1538, it was noted that there were seventy-two buildings on a site of some ninety-two acres, all enclosed within a precinct wall. However, less than half of the monastic buildings exist today (a large proportion of those being supported by scaffolding at this point in time), but the abbey still appears remarkably 'alive', with its richly decorated church largely in tact, and a wealth of history waiting to be discovered amongst the foundation stones of religious life over four centuries.

There is a terrace, owned by the National Trust, which runs along the eastern edge of the abbey and provides a wonderful vantage point for viewing the whole site from above. Even though there was a brief glimpse of the sun, conditions underfoot were still extremely wet and muddy so we didn't venture 'upwards' on this occasion.

The day was becoming darker by the minute, limiting Laurie's photographic opportunities to such an extent that we decided to 'call it a day' and head off back to the camp site for an early evening. After a cold and slightly disappointing day, we were looking forward to settling down with a bottle of good red, a few nibbles, and a half-decent TV programme to watch, and just let the day wash over us. Things didn't quite work out that way. Firstly, another motorhome had decided it liked the look of our pitch and was already set up for the night, so we had to park almost on top of the hikers in the dome tent. Then, after Laurie had hooked up to the electricity supply, switched on the gas supply and checked the water levels, he came inside to turn on the fire. Nothing! Despite numerous attempts to encourage it to ignite following the advised procedures, and several more employing the less orthodox methods of bashing it, and even swearing at it, the fire remained quite dead. With temperatures plummeting inside the van most evenings, this was a very serious situation which required immediate, remedial attention. After much patience, effort and concentration during which the unit and its component parts were dismantled and reassembled at least half a dozen times, it still refused to show any signs of an encouraging spark. More expletives, and derogatory remarks directed at the motorhome supplier, ensued, punctuated only with "That's it, we'll have to go home — we can't stay on the road without heating".

Me, I just calmly worked my way to the bottom of that bottle of red — purely in an attempt to keep warm, you understand — and offered the occasional acknowledgement that he was doing a sterling job! Eventually, Laurie's dogged determination resolved the problem, and our essential heating supply was turned up to 'full' whilst he related to me, for the umpteenth time, what he was going to say to the suppliers about their lack of quality control procedures, among other things!

With only one abbey on our schedule today, we enjoyed a more leisurely

Watercolour showing one of the spring houses at Mount Grace Priory

Mount Grace Priory — *North Yorkshire*
Crisp, white blossom masking the ancient tower of the small priory church

breakfast and showering routine, preferring to use our 'on board' shower in the relative warmth and comfort of our self-contained unit. Of course, the only disadvantage in both of us indulging in this luxury, is that the water storage tank needs refilling immediately, so 'someone' still has to get cold, and possibly wet, by standing outside to perform this task. Eventually, we completed the ritual 'tidy-up' routine inside, and the external maintenance of all facilities on the 'Swift', before heading south towards Fountains Abbey.

The journey would take us through the ancient City of Ripon, enabling us to stop briefly and look over the oldest cathedral in England, with its Anglo-Saxon crypt still in tact. As we entered Ripon Cathedral, the air was heavy with the smell of burning incense, a reminder that the Maundy service had only just finished. Already possessing more than its fair share of atmosphere, this heady aroma simply enhanced the spiritual beauty of this lovely church. It is an architectural delight, a sacred treasure and an historian's paradise. An outstanding example of 'small is beautiful'.

Walking through the thriving market in the centre of Ripon, we took the opportunity to buy some lovely fresh fruit and vegetables — in fact, two large bags of produce for a mere £3. What good value. We then noticed a stall selling every style, size and shape of picture frame, and found the perfect one for a sepia photograph we'd had taken at Beamish, dressed as a 'Sea Captain and Lady' in the early 1900s. A right pair of posers!

Now to the real work of the day and our second detailed exploration of the great Fountains Abbey — for us, the most evocative of all the ruined abbeys. Standing solitary and supreme in the steep-sided valley beside the River Skell, this hauntingly beautiful Cistercian abbey had completely captured my soul on our first visit two years ago and was, in fact, my inspiration for the book. That first glimpse on a cool, misty morning in November set my pulse racing and stirred my emotions to unbelievable depths.

Making our downhill approach to the abbey allowed Laurie to take several long-distance shots of the site which captured the full beauty of the surrounding grounds, with clusters of sunny primroses scattered along the banks, a few early bluebells bursting through the damp undergrowth, and a smattering of dainty, new blossom appearing on the trees. Nearing the abbey we saw an abundance of brightly-coloured wild flowers sprouting from the stately columns and arched windows, and tumbling down the Norman sandstone pillars of the nave. Here was a true sense of eternal life — all the new, young shoots springing from the heart of these ancient and long-redundant stones.

Before further investigation of the church, I just had to revisit the superb vaulted undercroft of the West Range — its sheer length and completeness, the almost claustrophobic stillness, and its eerie emptiness, sets the imagination

Byland Abbey — *North Yorkshire*
The remains of the south transept seen
through the beautiful west doorway

Rievaulx Abbey — *North Yorkshire*
Some of the ruinous walls given
a new lease of life with spring flowers

Rievaulx Abbey — *North Yorkshire*
The magnificent strength and power
of the presbytery columns

Ripon Cathedral — *North Yorkshire*
Just one of the many spectacular stained-
glass windows in this small cathedral

into overdrive. I almost **expected** an elderly, round-faced monk clad in his sombre habit, and chanting in whispered tones, to appear from behind one of the pillars! Emerging from the darkness, we systematically explored the remains of the great church and claustral buildings, the foundations of the infirmary and other outbuildings still in evidence, followed by a brisk walk along the river — specifically to obtain a 'few more angles' for Laurie's photographic bit! Apart from the abbey, the grounds at Studley Royal contain an early 18th Century water garden, Fountains Hall, and St Mary's Church in the deer park. It is quite easy to spend the best part of a beautiful day in this one place, especially if you come prepared with a picnic. However, even though it was dry today, there was a bitterly cold wind blowing and my hands, feet and nose were frozen, so we bypassed the other attractions and headed back to the van for some hot refreshment. That night proved to be extremely cold, and even wearing socks and T-shirts under the 13.5 tog duvet, did little to keep the blood circulating. We were now beginning to understand that only two temperature levels operated in the motorhome — very hot, or bloody freezing!

Following a disturbed night's sleep in the 'cold cabinet', we were in need of some serious warmth. A cooked breakfast, a mug of steaming tea, and the fire turned up to 'high' would do very nicely. However, this was the unfortunate moment we were about to discover that Calor gas was not condusive to arctic conditions, and had solidified overnight, resulting in a sparse and intermittent supply to both the cooker and fire! With several vigorous shakings, swapping over of gas bottles (and plenty of swearing), it became apparent that some improvisation was necessary. The question was "how could we heat up the frozen gas cylinders" — the solution was to take them over to the lukewarm showers, insert the obligatory 20p, and run them under the water for a while. Worth every penny! Having taken so long to get warm, we could not face hiking across to the site shower block again, and so made good use of our 'on board' facilities for the second morning running.

Splitting the driving between us on a 'day on day off' basis, it was my turn today, and I recalled the 'interesting' approach road to Kirkham Priory that I would have to navigate later in the motorhome. From what I remembered, even the average family car needed to proceed with extreme caution down the narrow 1 in 7 hill, around the sharp, blind bends and overgrown hedgerows. This was indeed going to test my driving skills to the limit.

An hour later, and having successfully completed my first challenge of the day, we crossed the old bridge over the River Derwent, which took us to the richly carved gatehouse entrance of the priory. The site looking ominously deserted, we parked the 'Swift' and consulted our guidebook to find that the opening time was 12 noon. With about forty-five minutes to kill, I put the kettle on while Laurie went 'walkabout' with his camera to find prospective shots from the opposite bank of the river. The English Heritage lady duly opened the gate at midday and gave us access to the remains of this Augustinian priory. As already mentioned, the 13th Century wide-arched gatehouse is a truly impressive sight, skillfully adorned with several heraldic shields still showing much of their intricate detail. There are also some wonderfully carved figures in canopied niches. Only the fragmented remains of several claustral buildings, and a single surviving block of the east front of the church, still stand as recognisable evidence of a busy, working priory. Sadly, for me, I feel it lacks that hallowed, 'monastic' atmosphere, possibly because so little of the church has survived, the 'heart' of the site had died. Nevertheless, what can be seen is architecturally ornate and, as I am reliably informed, very photogenic.

With our 'work' schedule completed for today, we now looked to 'List C' for inspiration. As Castle Howard was our nominated 'extra' for this area, and it had the advantage of being a place to explore under cover, we drove on to the early 18th Century palace built for the Earl of Carlisle. The prospect of being sheltered from the ever-threatening weather, and visiting somewhere we had not previously been, seemed like a good way to spend the afternoon.

Following lunch in the car park, we left the 'Swift' suitably attired in full waterproof gear, with an extra large brolly, and went in search of a bit of culture! After a tour of the house, we made our way to the cafeteria for a warming pot of tea and a piece of home-made cake while we pondered the possibility of inspecting the extensive grounds. It soon became apparent that this was not going to be a viable option, as we sat watching the persistent rain quickly changing into ever-increasing, white, fluffy blobs of snow swirling around in the prevailing wind. All the potential for yet another great Easter holiday!

Nothing for it now but to take a slow drive back to the camp site, have a decent meal, open a bottle and relax in our own ways — maybe do a bit of guitar practise, a bit of reading, watch the TV or whatever the mood dictates. For me, at least, whatever the activity it will be confined to 'indoors' though I suspect Laurie will brave the elements to 'have a pipe' — his own brand of relaxation!

Quite a full schedule today, with three abbeys on the agenda to visit, so we left Osmotherley reasonably early and set off in a north-westerley direction towards Richmond. A mile outside of the town, we took a minor road leading down, past the remains of the gatehouse, to arrive at Easby Abbey just as a watery, wintery-like sun was beginning to break through. The small, cobbled car park was deserted, leaving us ample space to manoeuvre the 'Swift' into a sheltered corner out of the way of most of the deep puddles, and offering some protection against the raw, gusting winds blowing through the valley.

Rievaulx Abbey — *North Yorkshire*
Standing on a high bank to appreciate the vastness of this once important abbey

Fountains Abbey — *North Yorkshire*
Approaching this enormous site from the southwest footpath

In common with the majority of these monastic sites, it was an extremely peaceful setting along the course of the River Swale where the only sounds audible were those of the birds' unbroken morning chorus. Although from first impressions there looks to be a good deal remaining of this Premonstratensian abbey, there is virtually nothing standing of the church, very little of the chapterhouse, and only fragmented walls and doorways of the other monastic buildings. The most complete area is the south range, where the frater still stands to almost its full height and retains its magnificent windows, one displaying some fine tracery. It was quite amusing to observe a couple of young rabbits scurrying back and forth along the latrine drains, obviously feeling safe and confident in the solitude of this ruinous maze.

Little appears to be known about the early history of Easby Abbey except that it was founded in the mid-12th Century by the Constable of Richmond Castle. By the time of the Dissolution in 1537, there were seventeen canons at the abbey.

Standing somewhat in its shadow, is a beautiful early Norman church — the Parish Church of St Agatha, which was in use even before the abbey was built. Inside the church are some wonderful 13th Century wall paintings depicting scenes from the Bible, still very detailed and colourful after seven hundred years.

Back inside the motorhome, Laurie having completed some routine cleaning of his camera equipment, now appeared to be engaged in some kind of jigsaw puzzle. It transpired that someone, probably in a supermarket car park, had punched a large hole in the offside rear light cover. Luckily all the broken fragments had fallen between the remaining cover and the bulb reflector unit, which allowed it to be reconstructed using some strong adhesive — and a considerable dose of patience! Meanwhile I took the opportunity of a dry moment to strip out the carpets and give them a good beating, sweep the floors, and brush out the mud and damp grass which had collected in the footwells. After a quick cup of tea, it was time to move on again.

We drove through Richmond, a delightful old market town dominated by an impressive castle, and picked up the A6108 which would lead us eventually to the ruins of Jervaulx Abbey. The name is a French style derivation from the original Yorevale — Vale of River Ure — and at the height of its wealth, the abbey owned half of the valley. Leaving the 'Swift' in the large car park opposite, we crossed the road and entered the privately-owned parkland, walking along the gravel path towards the small iron gate. Just inside the gate, past the monks' embalming slab, is a 'DIY' arrangement for the collection of entrance fees — an honesty box — which, hopefully, encourages visitors to make a donation towards the upkeep of this rambling, romantic site.

I sensed an untamed urgency to rediscover this enchanting ruin, with its

Fountains Abbey — *North Yorkshire*
The impressive undercroft of the west range

profusion of wild flowers bedecking the crumbling stone walls, and to feel the intense peace emanating from this old Cistercian monastery. Exactly one year ago we made our first visit to Jervaulx, on a gorgeous warm, sunny day and, although the weather had been appalling so far on this tour, we thought returning here might prove to be a lucky omen. For the first time since we began this tour, it hadn't actually rained, and the sun was shining through the fast-moving clouds for extended intervals. Laurie set off in earnest with his trusty camera, while I sat quite happily in a sheltered corner of the cloisters reflecting on life in the 13th Century. I tried to visualise where the monks would have spent their days undisturbed in hours of prayer and meditation, while the lay brothers would be labouring away relentlessly with the construction of this amazing abbey.

From its original dependence on Byland Abbey, Jervaulx became very prosperous, earning most of its income from sheep farming and the production of Wenslydale cheese, which the monks were forbidden to eat, but were "allowed to sell for a handsome profit".

At the Dissolution, Jervaulx suffered quite severely from mutilation at the hands of Henry VIII because Abbot Adam Sedbergh was supposedly implicated in the 'Northern Uprising', called the Pilgrimage of Grace. As a result, the perpetrators were executed, their monasteries were made an example of by being blown up by Thomas Cromwell's commissioners, and the stone was quarried off. With its turbulent history, it is remarkable that such substantial evidence can be seen today. Once again, this site leaves me feeling truly inspired, and absolutely relaxed with this inner sense of peace and calm engulfing my whole being. At this stage of the tour, I would have to nominate Jervaulx as one of my favourite abbey ruins.

Before leaving, we popped into the cafeteria and shop, situated in the car park, to buy a copy of the well-illustrated and informative guidebook on the abbey. We also enquired whether any china thimbles decorated with this picturesque ruin were available. Unfortunately, we were told none were made at present — a lucrative gap in the market, maybe!

Our intention now is to drive back up to the borders of County Durham to 'pick up' an abbey we had missed on our route down to North Yorkshire. Firstly, and most importantly, I suggested we might stop off somewhere for a decent lunch, as we had been 'on the go' for the past five hours and I was feeling quite faint through lack of food! An appropriate pub was located (with a car park big enough to accommodate the 'Swift'), and we satisfied our hunger with the most enormous Yorkshire puddings filled with sausages and onions in a thick, rich gravy — absolutely delicious. With our 'tums' almost bursting, we left the warm, sociable atmosphere of this local pub, where the 'lads' were heavily involved in the usual end of season football

Fountains Abbey — *North Yorkshire*
The powerful Norman nave columns glimpsed through the west doorway

Kirkham Priory — *North Yorkshire*
Ornate carving on the priory gatehouse

Kirkham Priory — *North Yorkshire*
Through the vaulted cloister entrance, the River Derwent flows along the site boundary

Easby Abbey — *North Yorkshire*
Detail along the west range guest chambers

scenarios, and made our way to Egglestone Abbey.

Remotely situated in the Pennine Hills, Egglestone was a Premonstratensian abbey colonized from Easby in the late 12th Century. It was one of the poorer houses, suffering severely from the frequent Scottish invasions and, as a result, very little remains in situ. The harsh, bland stonework of the church is accentuated by its bleak and exposed position above the River Tees. Even Laurie was struggling to capture an 'atmospheric shot' on film, but he did manage to search out the odd bit of bar-tracery in the lancet windows of the south transept, and an unusual five-bar mullioned window at the east end of the church.

The whole of the east range was restored in the late 16th Century to provide a dwelling house, and we had to look carefully amongst the Elizabethan conversion work to see any monastic evidence. We'd been blown across the site for about twenty minutes when a hailstorm forced us to take cover in the undercroft of the reredorter. From our sheltered position, watching the hail instantly turn to driving sleet, we could easily imagine the severity of life for the canons housed here some eight centuries ago.

With no sign of the weather improving, we battled against the strong winds and driving sleet on our downhill trek back to the 'Swift'. Discarding the snow boots, thermal gloves, fleece hat and rainproof gear, I did the only sensible thing we English do in the circumstances — put the kettle on for a piping hot cup of tea! Laurie, on the other hand, was determined to play with the camera beside the fast-flowing river to get some 'special effect' photographs — now here's a man who takes his work seriously!

Thoroughly disappointed at having made this long detour for such little reward due to the ghastly weather, we turned the 'Swift' around, drove off over the old toll bridge and headed into the town of Barnard Castle. Although a couple of miles in the wrong direction for our return journey to Osmotherley, Laurie thought while we were this close, I might be able to purchase a thimble that had escaped us on a previous visit here, due to half-day closing. I think he hates to miss an opportunity to add to my ever-growing collection almost as much as I do!

After dinner that evening, we sat and watched the steadily falling snow and wondered what we would wake up to the next morning.

Peeping out from beneath the duvet, we opened the curtain at the small window above the cab and beheld a typical Christmas card scene, with the glistening snow covering the valley like a heavy dusting of icing sugar. But it wasn't December, it was Easter Sunday! Our breath misty in the freezing air, hands and toes numb, we wasted no time in dressing in our warmest tracksuits (with extra jumpers underneath), and again went through the routine of coaxing some gas from the bottles. Over breakfast we discussed our itinerary for the day, and I began to get the most surreal feeling; it was bitterly cold, there was snow on the ground, gale force winds rocking the van with a vengeance, and we were calmly planning our route over to the Northeast coastal town of Whitby! Was this just another facet of the great adventure, or had we lost it completely? Whatever enthusiasm I had started this tour with, had recently become buried due to the prevailing meteorological factors, and I was now struggling to overcome those feelings and find the grit and determination required to get the job done.

The rigid routine maintenance programme for the 'Swift' had to be curtailed this morning due to the frozen condition of the water taps which, in turn, meant we had to be even more frugal with the remaining fresh water supply on board. It was all these minor inconveniences and problems we were experiencing first-hand (that we had been completely oblivious to in the planning stages), that were slowly chipping away at our tolerance levels, and were causing frustration to set in.

In any event, we were on the road by 8.45 a.m., having planned a stop at Gisborough en route to Whitby. We arrived at the town car park and had walked up the street towards the boundary wall, separating the parish church from the old Augustinian priory, without seeing a soul. The entrance gate was padlocked so we continued through the churchyard and came across a public park with a footpath that ran parallel to the back wall of the priory grounds. From this vantage point we were able to see the full glory of the huge east end of the church, the only part of the building still standing to its full height. Anxious to explore the site in closer detail, we walked back to the entrance and were pleased to notice that the gates were now open.

On entering this pretty site, the foreboding, dark ashlar stonework surrounding the enormous central window of the east end, presented a striking contrast to the frontage of tidy lawns, interspersed with large clumps of daffodils, and neat, colourful flower borders. The window, some 56ft high, provided a perfect frame for the scenic backdrop of rolling hills in the distance. It was obvious why the eastern gable of the church was left in tact as a 'feature' when the remainder of the site was landscaped in the early 18th Century, but I often wonder at the rationale behind the wilful destruction of such architectural beauty and heritage purely to provide 'romantic ruins'.

A mansion built on the site was subsequently demolished in 1825 and the owner, Admiral Chaloner, began excavations for other monastic evidence. Today we can see the results of his work; the bases of three nave columns, much of the original foundations and a barrel vaulted passage. A large section of the original Norman gatehouse also survives, mainly because it was retained

Jervaulx Abbey — ***North Yorkshire***
Early aubretia and tangled roots spread across the rubbled walls

Jervaulx Abbey — *North Yorkshire*
Looking at the remains of the monastic dormitory

Jervaulx Abbey — *North Yorkshire*
*Among the numerous wild flowers, beautiful cowslips
can be found mingling with the crumbling stones*

as a gatehouse-cum-porters lodge for the later mansions built. Although the site does not have too many 'exploratory' options, it is a pleasant, peaceful spot, ideal for 'vegging out' on a balmy afternoon.

With the sky above looking extremely grim, the wind whipping fiercely across the exposed roads, and the faintest suggestion of snow about, we were beginning to doubt our earlier decision to visit Whitby Abbey. On the other hand, we'd come this far so 'in for a penny, in for a pound'. Soon we were in the bustling seaside town and could see the haunting, grey abbey silhouetted against a threatening, black sky as it stood proudly on its headland above the harbour. However, it took us another thirty minutes to actually reach the site, having circumnavigated the town a further three times, following a series of confused directions, and then going back out along the road for two miles to find a narrow lane (not signposted) which looked as though it would lead us to the abbey. Indeed, at the end of the lane was a brand-new corporation car park with good access to the ruins of this splendid Benedictine abbey.

By this time it was virtually impossible to see the abbey — which was only about 300yds in front of us — because we were caught in a severe blizzard, reducing visibility to almost zero. The gusting winds were so strong that the heavily falling snow was coming at the 'Swift' horizontally, and we were becoming nervous about the stability of the vehicle against such conditions. So much so, in fact, that Laurie decided it was prudent to turn the van to face into the wind to reduce the violent rocking and swaying sensation — it really was quite horrendous! As we sat there drinking a mug of hot, strong Assam, we recalled our visit to Whitby just eighteen months ago. What a contrast — it was a perfect late autumn day, the warm sun reflecting the wonderful orange tones of the abbey's stonework and a deep azure sky above, completing the idyllic picture.

Now we hurriedly dressed in our warmest garments and full protective outdoor gear, to attempt a brisk 'walkabout' before the next squall of wintery weather, came in from over the sea. The biting winds and slippery, sodden conditions underfoot, were not exactly conducive to creative thoughts and an enthusiastic investigation of the site on this occasion. Nevertheless, it was difficult not to be impressed and inspired by the extensive monastic ruins with fine examples of the Gothic and Early English style architecture, dating from the 13th Century. It has been the site of religious houses for over one thousand years, and an earlier priory was once the third wealthiest Benedictine house in Yorkshire.

We did manage to cover the entire site just as the next snow-laden clouds were positioning themselves above us, once again threatening to drop their load. Laurie was particularly disappointed because this striking ruin is so photographic in the right conditions, especially the superb east front of the

Egglestone Abbey — *Co Durham*
An arched doorway, with a traceried window
above, on the south wall of the nave

Osmotherley — *North Yorkshire*
The scene that greeted us on
Easter Sunday in North Yorkshire

Whitby Abbey — *North Yorkshire*
Looking into the presbytery arcade
to see the magnificent detail
and colours of the sandstone columns

Sawley Abbey — *Lancashire*
Fragmented abbey remains
through a surviving archway

church, but even with all the technical equipment he possessed, the bad light, the wind and the snow, were proving too much to cope with today.

Struggling back to the motorhome, wet cold and exhausted from the physical effort of constant battling against the wind, we now had to give some thought as to how we would spend the rest of the day. Gradually eliminating the List C options open to us, we decided to 'give in gracefully' and go for something warm, cosy, restful — and sensible! Hence, an hour later we were parked in a layby at the highest point on the North Yorkshire Moors, the roast dinner cooking, the gas fire on full, and the TV tuned in preparation for watching the Argentinian Grand Prix. Settling down on the settee with a large glass of full-bodied Rioja, we whiled away the next three hours in the simulated comforts of a Sunday afternoon at home. Easter Sunday was certainly going to be a memorable day in many respects.

Back at base — our last night at Osmotherley — it was, unbelievably, the first dry, bright evening we'd experienced since the beginning of our tour. Laurie took great pleasure in having a late stroll around the site, smoking his pipe, and watching the playful antics of the young rabbits as they scampered between and under the cars and caravans, even though I'd cajoled him into supervising the pile of washing and drying to be done in the launderette! I got down to some serious strumming practise with the guitar after much re-tuning, probably due to the extreme temperatures in the 'Swift'. All in all a much better end to the day than we could have envisaged first thing that morning.

Awoken at some ungodly hour by the continuous squawking of the resident pheasants, I lifted the window shutters to reveal a glorious, sunny morning with a cloudless blue sky. How, in such a relatively short space of time, can the weather change so dramatically? But I'm not complaining — this change I can cope with. What a difference it makes being able to get ourselves, and the van, organised in dry conditions, and how much more light-hearted and enthusiastic we feel about the prospect of today's historical visits.

Our first destination will be Bolton Abbey in the west of Yorkshire. In fact, the remains are of an Augustinian priory — never granted the status of an abbey — picturesquely set beside the River Wharfe in the extensive grounds of the Duke of Devonshire. We were both praying the weather would hold as we'd only visited Bolton once before, on a dull and overcast day, and we were looking forward to seeing the full glory of the abbey on a bright, spring day. Pulling into the large (expensive) Strid car park, we collected all the necessary gear and set off on the short walk through the village before arriving at the 'hole-in-the-wall' entrance. We were not disappointed — the sun shone, the scenery was spectacular, and the ruins were delightful. The only consideration we had to contend with, were the hordes of hikers frequenting the site, obviously out enjoying the Bank Holiday Monday sunshine after

A moody watercolour of Whitby Abbey showing the great, east end in its exposed location

being confined to their homes by the 'winter weekend'.

This priory has an interesting history and, like most, was built in stages, dependant on the prevailing conditions at the time — poverty, invasion, severe weather, sickness — resulting in the west tower never reaching completion before the Dissolution. However, the magnificent mid-13th Century nave of the priory church was kept in tact and is still in use, with much restoration, as the local parish church. Of the ruins, it is the east end gable which has survived to its full height and a substantial section of the north transept. To gain a better perspective of the site, we crossed the river via the wooden footbridge, not quite as exciting as the stepping stones strategically placed in the fast-flowing river, but certainly a safer bet for keeping dry! Climbing the banks opposite, we surveyed a glorious scene with the river flowing past in the foreground, the pretty, little graveyard at the centre, and the beautiful monastic ruins in the distance, all encompassed in fabulous, rolling countryside. Absolutely perfect. Of course, Laurie wasted no opportunities with the camera, clicking contentedly for well over an hour — he must have snapped every conceivable inch of the site from every aspect — above, below, from this angle and that angle, with this tree or those flowers, with and without the river! This was now getting close to how we imagined it would be — me sitting contentedly beside the river gathering my thoughts to put into words, and him checking out all the creative, photographic possibilities to produce that outstanding picture.

Our guardian angel must have been watching over us that morning because we had successfully completed our task and were on our way back to the motorhome before the onset of more drizzly rain and darkening skies. As we had paid the compulsory full-day rate to park the 'Swift' here, we took full advantage of it by remaining to cook our lunch of lamb chops, while contemplating our plans for the rest of the day. Originally, the plan had been to visit Bolton and then drive across to Sawley Abbey in the afternoon. However, we had made up some time, due to our early start this morning, and decided that we could now include some research on the nearby Skipton Castle. Therefore, after lunch we set off along the A59, but about half a mile outside of Skipton, we joined a continuous stream of traffic and had second thoughts about this being a good idea. The town was heaving, the car parks were full, and the motorists were becoming more intolerant as they sat in endless, stationary queues. It would have been a difficult enough task trying to find sufficient space to park the normal family saloon somewhere in the vicinity, but with a 20ft motorhome it was absolutely impossible.

With a wistful look at the castle's boundary wall as we crawled back out of the town, we now made our way to the Lancashire border village of Sawley. Some thirty minutes later, we had parked the 'Swift' on the opposite side of the road to the Cistercian abbey site (known as Salley in the Middle Ages).

We were immediately struck by the dramatic industrial backdrop to the ruins, and the dark, barren hills stretching far into the distance. From excavations early in the 19th Century, it is easy to distinguish the layout of the abbey but, apart from the church with its short aisleless nave, not much stands above foundation level. There were several small areas of mosaic tiling across the site, and evidence of the monks' night stairs in the south transept. But even with so little surviving of the great abbeys that once stood so proudly on these sites, there is always the odd, beautifully carved corbel, a wonderfully decorative archway, a surviving piscina that takes you by surprise or, as here, some beautifully preserved medieval floor tiles worthy of more than a passing glance. If there is nothing visible to catch your imagination, there is usually something of interest to read about in the abbey's often-chequered history.

As day twelve draws to a close, we get back in the motorhome and drive again into Yorkshire to find our overnight stopping place at Otley. This turned out to be an extremely long and tedious drive along the minor roads, swamped with Bank Holiday traffic, and I was becoming less than amenable as the journey continued. However, when we reached the small farm site, it was like a breath of fresh air, with the pitches (all hardstanding) set high above the main A65 and some spectacular views across Wharfedale.

Laurie commenced with the setting up of the van to enable us to settle down for the evening. As so often is proved the case, there was a minor technical hitch — no power coming from the 240v electrical hook-up. The fuses appeared to be OK at our junction box, so Laurie went off in search of the farmer for his assistance in tracking down the problem. Fifteen to twenty minutes later, having seen the pair of them clambering across a huge tractor barn, the offending distribution box was located and the appropriate breaker switch turned on. By the time he returned, I was several glasses into a bottle of red — my solution to these minor irritations!

Tuesday dawned bright and crisp with just a hint of fresh snow capping the distant hills. This location was so delightful that we were reluctant to 'pack up and go', knowing that we would be driving into the busy outskirts of Leeds later that morning to face the world returning to work after the Easter break. Even more distressing was the fact that over the next three days we had planned to visit no less than five City centres along our route to further our research work on England's cathedrals.

Quite surprisingly the roads were not that busy, and we arrived at Kirkstall Abbey just before 10.00 a.m. In its unusual urban environment, this austere Cistercian abbey with its cold, blackened stone, sits in a well-maintained council park. This is the most complete Cistercian monastery in England, and because no substantial alterations have been carried out since its original

Bolton Abbey — *North Yorkshire*
The priory dominates this stretch of the valley beside the River Wharfe

completion in the mid-12th Century, it is an ideal opportunity to understand the typical layout and accommodation provided by a medieval monastery.

It was disappointing to find that the only parts of the abbey accessible to the public were the cloister and chapterhouse, all other entrances being barred by heavily padlocked, wrought-iron gates, and the entire site enclosed by fencing. Employing some alternative and imaginative means, Laurie managed to obtain a few reasonable shots of the more interesting aspects of this site. Sadly though, he was unable to focus on the detailed carvings and the numerous statues we could see because of an abundance of foliage or other obstacles in prominent positions between him and the subject. After we'd walked the perimeter of the site, straining to see as much of the magnificently preserved monastic buildings as was possible, we crossed the busy main road in front of the abbey to call into the museum, originally the abbey gatehouse. Here we were fortunate to buy a detailed layout and guide to Kirkstall Abbey, for the princely sum of 50p, as well as a lovely china thimble — another one to add to that fast-growing collection!

Now for a real challenge. York City Centre during school half-term holidays. I could just picture it — traffic probably at a standstill, car parks overflowing, hundreds of family groups shopping and even more tourists milling around the historical attractions of the City than was usual. However, York Minster is on our itinerary for today, and we will attempt to cover it. Consulting our 'guide to City car parks without height barriers', we found a convenient 'Park and Ride' a couple of miles outside York and agreed that this would be our only hope of getting near the place.

It was exactly as I'd imagined, but worse! The immense cathedral was awash with people admiring its Gothic architecture, its wonderful chapterhouse, its magnificent choir and Lady Chapel and so much more. Laurie waited patiently — sometimes for several minutes — to be able to take 'the right shot'. I think it had something to do with slow shutter speeds, using a tripod, and waiting for people to disappear behind columns, or other places where they would be obscured from the frame. It all sounded very technical to me! I was left, as usual, looking after all his excess 'baggage' while I sat and lost myself in the mesmeric atmosphere of this beautiful feat of craftsmanship.

With the volume of people continually entering the cathedral, Laurie's job of collecting good library photographs was becoming ever more difficult. He decided to give in gracefully, knowing we would be able to return on a less busy occasion to finish the work, and we went outside into the bustling City streets. We had planned to go to the Jorvik Centre, but one look at the queue was enough for him to suggest that we return immediately to the motorhome and head for somewhere less hectic!

Kirkstall Abbey — *West Yorkshire*
The amazingly complete old abbey church resting behind the fresh
pink blossom of one of the many trees in this parkland setting

Our stopover for this evening was a short distance outside of Selby, with the aim of visiting the abbey early the following morning. As it was only mid-afternoon, and we were now at a loose end, we thought we might as well gain a couple of hours on tomorrow's schedule and visit the abbey on our way to the camp site.

Selby was the first monastery to be founded in Northern England following the Norman Conquest and much of its solid Norman architecture is still in evidence. The abbey's building programme spanned some 130 years and became one of the most influential in Yorkshire, after York itself. The lovely Abbey Church survives today as the Parish Church of Selby. Laurie, quite satisfied that he had been able to photograph plenty of the splendid detail, suggested that it was time to search out the camp site for this evening's stopover.

As with many of the quieter, certified locations, the site took a bit of finding, but we did eventually arrive at the farmyard entrance just as darkness fell. As the 'Swift' was cautiously manoeuvred around the tractors, trailers and giant hay bales, a kind soul appeared from behind a shed and directed us to the golf clubhouse for registration. Avoiding as many of the larger, slurry-filled potholes as possible, we managed to park the van almost at the clubhouse entrance. Snow was falling heavily by now, and we made a quick dash for the inviting warmth of the bar. This proved to be a real winner with us — check into the site, have a hot toddy, order some dinner, and lounge on a comfy sofa in front of the roaring, log fire. Feeling that wonderful heaviness that comes with eating, drinking and relaxing in a congenial atmosphere, we felt it wise to make a move now before we drifted into sleep. Pulling on our snowboots and coats to venture forth, once again, into the arctic conditions of this Yorkshire farmyard, we soon had the 'Swift' neatly parked on a firm base for the night.

Overnight, the temperature had noticeably risen a few degrees, because the only evidence of yesterday's snowfall were the waterlogged fields and the ever-deepening, sludgy puddles surrounding us. By late morning we decided to face the prospect of yet another wet, grey and hazy day — if we hadn't known differently, we could have been fooled into thinking this to be a typical November day! Notwithstanding the depressing conditions, I refused to feel downhearted today, because we were on our way to visit my favourite cathedral, and it wasn't in a big city.

Our journey took us in an easterly direction to Beverley, where we would find the spectacular Minster, a cathedral in all but name. I can recall vividly this remarkably decorative church, constructed of lovely soft-toned sandstone and built in the early English style, and its many treasures revealed inside. Today, however, there was time only for a brief reconnoitre to take the relevant library photographs, and refresh our memories with its timeless charm.

The 'Swift'

York Minster — **York**
The fabulous rose window in the south transept

Overwhelmed by Beverley Minster's breathtaking beauty, the aura of inspiration and hope, and its enchanting atmosphere, I can sense many more opportunities will be taken to visit this remarkable church.

Reluctantly, we left Beverley and Yorkshire, and drove southbound over the Humber Bridge and into Lincolnshire. Our overnight stop would be just outside of Market Rasen at a commercial caravan park. The only other option we had was the CC site at the racecourse but, because of a mid-week meeting, the venue was fully booked. Not being enthusiasts for 'the Sport of Kings', we simply had no idea just how many racecourses there were scattered throughout the country. It had almost become an obsession with us to look out for them along every road we travelled!

Starting off early again this morning, we hoped to get into the City of Lincoln before the traffic, and parking, became too horrendous. Actually, it was pleasantly quiet for the rush hour, and we arrived at the coach park beside the castle's boundary walls before nine o'clock. As we approached the west front of Lincoln Cathedral, Laurie was delighted to find that much of the scaffolding, that had smothered the building on our previous visit, had now been removed. This fact alone would improve the photographic opportunities immensely, so I was advised!

Even though I love to visit all the cathedrals, in common with everyone else, I have my favourites, and 'the others'. Lincoln, in my opinion, feels huge, cold and inexplicably void of atmosphere, although it does boast some magnificent architecture. The unusual feature of this cathedral, not being of monastic foundation, are the cloisters, which simply provide a covered walkway, and a perfect burial place for the deceased bishops.

Following our internal explorations, we ventured back outside to walk along the south side of the cathedral, where we found the entrance to the remains of the medieval Bishop's Palace. This was a sizeable, and fairly impressive site, built on several terraces as it sprawled down the hill. Having sufficiently broadened our historical, and ecclesiastical, knowledge of the ancient City of Lincoln, we were content to press on with the day's itinerary.

Our next stop was in the pleasant, market town of Southwell in Nottinghamshire, where we would be retracing our steps to visit the delightfully, small-scale cathedral. Southwell Minster is probably the least known of the English cathedrals, but it is a strong contender for the category of 'once seen, never forgotten'. It has a strong, bland external appearance, due to the square Norman towers capped with their original lead spires, which provide a very distinct and unusual feature. For such a compact cathedral, Southwell carries an almost unassuming beauty and elegance throughout, completely belying the austere, Norman architecture. Laurie

Selby Abbey — *West Yorkshire*
Looking from the choir to the east window

was more than pleased with his photographic session here, and shortly joined me in the refectory to enjoy a hot, elderberry cordial, before venturing into town for some shopping. I find it continually distressing to have to accommodate such mundane chores into our daily schedules, especially, when I'm feeling particularly elated after visiting such an inspirational site. Oh well, I suppose there has to be a down side to every 'up'.

Momentarily losing all sense of direction from the town back to the 'Swift', we strode through a labyrinth of narrow streets, until we came across the main road outside the cathedral where we had parked. Before finally leaving Southwell, we tried to see if it was possible to explore the ruins of the Archbishop's Palace, but unfortunately they did not appear to be open to the public.

With a reasonably short drive ahead, through Lincolnshire to the borders of Cambridgeshire, we stayed away from the major roads and took a 'cross-country' trek. We were becoming slightly alarmed at the amount of water lying in the fields, some areas so large that they resembled lakes. As we drove on, we also noticed several rivers had burst their banks, and it was only then that we recalled having heard on the radio about the severe flooding throughout Wales and Central England. Always thinking ahead, Laurie immediately telephoned the camp site at Market Deeping to enquire whether they had been affected by the floods, or if they were still able to accommodate us for the night. Apparently about three-quarters of the site was submerged, but we were reliably advised that there was some firm ground at the far corner of the site for us to park the motorhome.

When we arrived at the camp site, which looked like an incredibly muddy bog in the early evening darkness, we were directed to the higher ground and told to park on the firm, gravel road. Although the 'Swift' was stable enough on this base, it was a weird sensation looking out and seeing nothing but water surrounding us — it had certain similarities to being marooned on our own little island! Luckily there was no overnight rain, but Laurie still had to wade knee-high across the pitch which, in full daylight gave the appearance more of a paddy field than a caravan site, to disconnect the electrics and fill up with fresh water. We've certainly had our fair share of 'exciting' weather on this trip!

With another, potentially busy, City to visit, we managed to leave the site without any undue problems, despite the surplus mud and water, and travelled into Peterborough. We had visited the cathedral at the same time last year, and knew exactly where the nearest open parking area, without height barriers, was situated — we also knew it was quite a long walk from that car park to the cathedral and prayed the weather might just stay dry for a couple of hours.

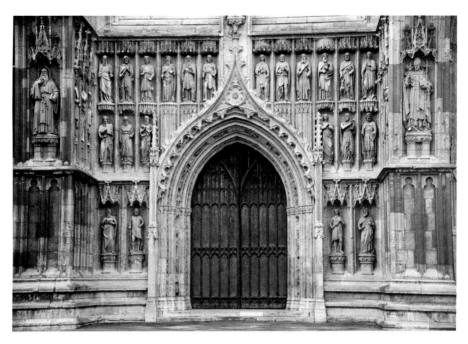

Beverley Minster — *East Riding*
The impressively decorative west front and doorway

Lincoln Cathedral — *Lincolnshire*
The east end glimpsed from across the green

Another well-thought out plan that was perfectly executed: the parking was trouble-free, the weather was drab but dry, and Laurie was able to take the library photographs he'd hoped without too many obstructions. The most fascinating aspects of Peterborough Cathedral, especially from a photographic viewpoint, are the exquisitely painted ceilings, and as I knew it was liable to be a long job, I politely excused myself and spent some time browsing through the market — conveniently situated between the cathedral and the car park!

By 10.30 a.m., the research work for the day was done, and we now had the rest of the day 'free' to visit a couple of sites from our List C locations. Since his schooldays, Laurie has had something of a fascination for archaeological digs and likes to investigate such sites as are accessible to the general public. Bearing this in mind, we drove a little way outside of Peterborough to Flag Fen, a Bronze Age settlement that has been excavated over the last twenty-five years with some amazing finds. We spent an absorbing, but very damp, two hours walking across this settlement and learning about life some three thousand years ago.

Moving across Cambridge and up through Norfolk, we found our next destination just off the coast of The Wash. About four miles from King's Lynn, a sturdy, rectangular keep, surrounded by massive earthworks, forms the remains of Castle Rising. This fine mid-12th Century domestic keep, still standing to its full height, provided excellent accommodation for royalty and distinguished guests throughout the ages, among them the infamous Queen Isabella. Many of the internal rooms retain their original features, and this, as well as delving into the 'royal' history of the castle, made for a really interesting visit.

As we could see the village, from our high position on the edge of the castle's defensive earthworks, we decided to take a stroll and have a closer look. It was a pretty little place with some wonderful cottages and an abundance of 'old-fashioned' gardens brimming with colour. A typical 'one pub, one general store-cum-post office, and a church', in the middle of nowhere, sleepy Norfolk village. Delightful.

Back on the road again, and a short distance away lies the vast Sandringham Estate, which will be our base for the next three nights. The caravan club site here was first-class: extremely well laid out, with plenty of room between pitches and exceptionally clean and tidy. Our only immediate concern, after checking in at reception, was that no hardstanding pitches were available on our first night. With the widespread flooding we'd recently experienced, we proceeded with caution in choosing a close-cut grass pitch. The ground seemed quite firm, and within minutes we were pitched, 'hooked up' and fully operational.

Armed with a purse full of coins, I got Laurie to lug a large, heavy bag of dirty washing over to the launderette, to start putting it through its cycle while we had dinner. This was another of those really boring, everyday chores like the shopping, that had to be attended to on a regular basis, and 'built' into the grand plan, dependent on timing and available facilities. Needless to say, so far things have worked out with clockwork precision — and I wouldn't have accepted anything less from my former Project Manager!

Watching the TV weather forecast for today, it promised a much drier, brighter day, which is why we were planning to drive through previously unexplored countryside in an attempt to find a couple of Norfolk's lesser known, remote religious houses. However, as is generally the case, the forecast was totally wrong, and what we had in prospect was an atrociously wet and gloomy day. Although we were now nearly three weeks into this trip, and thought we had accepted the cold, wet and windy conditions as the 'norm', we were about to discover that our inner frustrations were lurking dangerously below a fairly calm surface. A bit like a grumbling volcano, that lies dormant for great periods of time, then one day almost out of the blue, erupts into a violent, seething mass of fire and molten lava.

Seemingly unperturbed by the weather, we theoretically planned our drive to Walsingham Abbey, via Creake Abbey and Binham Priory. This would effectively take us on a circular route, finishing close to the main A148 and the road back to Sandringham at the end of the day. Setting off along the coastal road towards Wells-next-the-Sea, we quite easily found our first destination, Creake Abbey, but unfortunately were not able to park the motorhome in the safe knowledge that we'd be able to drive it off the sodden grass again. After weighing up the situation, we agreed to move on to Binham and backtrack to Creake later that day in the hope that weather conditions might improve. The nightmare was about to commence. What looked to be a reasonably straightforward journey of no more than ten miles, albeit along a few minor, twisty roads, turned out to be an hour long fiasco caught in a dense network of narrow lanes that bore no resemblance whatsoever to our map. Moreover, the rain was absolutely relentless, resulting in substantial surface water, and half the topsoil from surrounding fields being washed down the lanes, which caused the 'Swift' to ski along the road rather precariously.

Accusations about map-reading skills were tossed in the air, remarks suggesting the doubtful parentage of certain 'weathermen' were banded about freely, and Laurie's driving abilities, along with his usual composure, were deteriorating by the minute! Our tempers now extremely frayed at the edges, Laurie made one too many of his derogatory remarks aimed in my direction, and I bit back so ferociously, I almost frightened myself. Enough was enough — I wanted to go home, AND RIGHT NOW!

Selby Abbey — *West Yorkshire*
The ornately carved north porch
with its 'secret room' above

Southwell Minster — *Nottinghamshire*
Looking down the nave
to the central organ and the east end

Taking me at my word, he swung the motorhome through a complete 180 degrees, and drove with silent determination through the never-ending maze of tiny roads, until he stumbled across a main road heading south. About forty-five minutes into this helter-skelter journey, we approached the first town of any significance and I decided it was time to make my move. I "politely" asked him to stop the vehicle in the 'out of town' lorry park and, armed with large umbrella, all the credit cards and cash (I never leave him in charge of the money), I strode off up the road. Arriving in the centre of Swaffham, I began to wonder exactly what my next move was to be. First I needed to get out of this rain, and a quaint coffee shop beckoned me in to take shelter, and give me time to compose my thoughts. I was angry, upset, cold, and drenched through in these monsoon conditions and what I wanted more than anything at this moment was the comfort and security of my own home. Then I saw across the street the Tourist Information Bureau. There was the answer — I'd find the time of the next train to London and be on my way.

Without going into a protracted account of what followed, all I'm prepared to say is that Swaffham no longer has a railway station, the next coach didn't leave until the following morning, and that left me having to walk back to the 'Swift' with my tail between my legs. I hadn't even considered the possibility that Laurie might have driven off without me — although he told me afterwards he was only going to give me an hour to return before he made a move, but with no money he almost certainly didn't have sufficient diesel to make the journey home.

In the middle of the car park we had a real 'nose to nose' confrontation, with a tirade of verbal accusations and denials on both sides, and some over-zealous gesticulations that would have caused mild amusement from any onlookers. At the peak of this uncharacteristic outbreak of mild hysteria, we both collapsed into a fit of nervous laughter. Not realising how mentally exhausted we had become with the frustration, and pent-up emotions of the last three weeks, this outburst had cleared the air, and we now felt more determined than ever that nothing would prevent us from completing what we'd set out to achieve.

Now finding ourselves somewhat further south than had been originally planned, and having not successfully visited any of our sites for the day, we now re-visited our itinerary to work out the most efficient way of covering all intended destinations.

Our sanity now restored, we agreed not to let the worst April weather on record, defeat our plans for the rest of the day, and resolved to visit Castle Acre Priory (now only four miles away) which we were supposed to visit tomorrow. Remaining optimistic that the rain would ease sufficiently for us to venture outside soon, we sat in the large car park at the priory and enjoyed a late lunch while we waited. I'm not sure to this day if the sky did actually lighten, and the torrential rain turn to a fine drizzle, or if it was simply a case of mind over matter. In any event, we walked the extensive, ruinous site, and Laurie took several shots with the tripod, hoping to offset the poor light conditions, and we had a thoroughly enjoyable visit. There is an awful lot to be said for 'clearing the air', as long as it doesn't get out of hand!

The history of this Cluniac priory, thought to have been constructed late 11th/early 12th Century, is quite sketchy but, in common with many abbeys and priories, it is known to have suffered financial difficulties and the odd scandal with supposed 'vagabond' monks. From the ruins of the church displaying some elaborate blind arcading on its impressive west front, to the adjacent western range and prior's lodging house with its unusual chequerboard pattern of ashlar and dressed flint work on the exterior wall above its arched entrance, there is much worthy of closer inspection. Along the southern boundary of the site, runs a small water channel, once serving as the latrine, but now banked with a varied display of wild flowers. Unfortunately, in today's rapidly fading light conditions, we did not see the full glory of the flintwork, or the true, natural beauty of the colourful flowers scrambling over the walls of this delightful priory.

It was now 3.30 in the afternoon and we were not looking forward to returning to our camp site to face the prospect of yet another long, wet, windy and cold evening. Consequently, we took a bit of a detour and drove to Oxburgh Hall, a 15th Century moated, manor house now in the care of the National Trust. Although neither of us are especially 'into' old manor houses or stately homes, with rooms full of period furniture and art collections, our decision was based on clinical facts; it would be dry; it would be somewhere different; and it would mean we would spend less time sitting around in the motorhome that evening. As it happened, the history of the house, and the Bedingfeld family, proved to be more interesting than many, and the grounds, which included formal gardens, a 'wilderness walk' and a woodland area, were delightful. There is also a small 19th Century Catholic Chapel containing a splendid altarpiece and some beautiful carved woodwork. However, for us, the *'pièce de résistance'* was the fascinating ruined church, outside the grounds of Oxburgh Hall, but accessible from the car park. Inside the ruined church was the Bedingfeld Chantry Chapel, the burial place for many members of the family until the end of the 18th Century. Almost the entire parish church was destroyed in 1948 with the collapse of the steeple but, amazingly, the chantry suffered little damage, and its fine monuments and the magnificent early 16th Century Renaissance terracotta screens are a pure delight to behold.

More than satisfied that we'd managed to salvage at least part of a potentially disastrous day, we drove back to the Sandringham Estate via King's Lynn. We needed to withdraw some cash and, at the same time, thought we might

Peterborough Cathedral — *Cambridgeshire*
The towering walls rise up to the beautifully painted ambulatory ceiling

Castle Acre Priory — *Norfolk*
A perfect example of Norman blind arcading on the west front

treat ourselves to a fish and chip supper. Having done a complete circuit of the town without passing either bank or building society, I accosted a 'local' for directions to the nearest cashpoint, and a 'take-away' chippie that was open at 6.30 on a Saturday evening! Not much to ask you'd think — but you would be wrong. This kindly soul actually offered to walk with me right across town to where all the banks are located, and at the same time gave me the 'gen' on the non-availability of fast food in this town. It seemed our only chance of enjoying a decent bit of cod 'n chips was to drive to a little village the other side of Sandringham, where there was liable to be a waiting period as they only 'cooked to order'.

My friendly informant came up trumps — not only was the supper extremely good, but there was ample parking space opposite for the motorhome, which enabled Laurie to prepare all the accompaniments, such as bread and butter, a pot of strong tea, etc., while I was queuing. An unexpectedly relaxed and pleasant end to a day that began so explosively!

Waking to the sun streaming through the roof vents, and with all yesterday's tensions a fading memory, we decided to try and recreate Saturday's itinerary. By reversing the order of our visits, and travelling to Walsingham first, we found a route with slightly better roads. Eventually we found the tiny village and, with difficulty, managed to manoeuvre the 'Swift' through the narrow streets to the coach park on the outskirts. Equipped with all the usual photographic paraphernalia, we hiked back down to the religious centre of this quiet, Norfolk haven. There were chapels, churches and halls of every denomination, and the High Street was saturated with quaint shops selling an assortment of Catholic artefacts, 'holy' souvenirs and biblical reading material. Given this environment, and the fact it was Sunday, we were dismayed to find the abbey ruins closed — not open until 10.00 a.m. the following day!

Next stop on the agenda was the elusive Binham Priory, approximately five miles from Walsingham according to our map. Some twenty miles later, having driven down single-track lanes, been barred by numerous 6' 6" width restriction signs, and circled the village at least three times without being able to gain entry, we finally agreed to let this particular ruin 'rest in peace'. With this omission, we completed the circuit and travelled on to Creake Abbey.

In its setting of absolute tranquillity, and with the late morning sun warming the old foundation stones, Creake looked a very different place to the one I remembered from yesterday's brief glimpse. This lowly Augustinian abbey, originally the site of an almshouse for the poor, suffered two traumas in its history which brought about its early suppression: in the mid 15th Century a disastrous fire destroyed the church and several of the monastic buildings and, at the beginning of the 16th Century, a fatal epidemic ended the community at Creake. The fragmented remains in their well-maintained grounds now provide a perfect place for the contemplation of life's simple, natural pleasures, listening to the gurgling stream as it tumbles along its journey; watching a pair of butterflies dancing through the flower-clad foundations; inhaling the rare, rich smells emanating from the neighbouring farms! Laurie was almost tempted to unearth the sketch pad and pencils, and bring his own creation to life on paper — but it was only 'almost'.

One thing that continued to bother us was our difficulty in understanding why we could not follow our route from the road map we were using. After some careful examination of the map, and now having a good knowledge of the roads in this area, it transpired that some of the traffic priorities had changed since our map had been printed. Satisfied that we were able to solve that little mystery, we now returned to Sandringham.

It was almost midday, and time to take advantage of our stay on the 7,000 acre estate with a visit to the vast country house, one of many private homes of Her Majesty the Queen. Following the usual 'gourmet lunch in a car park', we spent a wonderful afternoon exploring this impressive royal home, and the fabulous gardens. Originally bought for Albert Edward, the Prince of Wales in 1862, Sandringham remains a 'Royal' favourite, and today's family traditionally enjoy spending their Christmas in this superb, secluded location.

The restored, 16th Century church of St Mary Magdalene on the estate, is well worth a visit. This fine carrstone country church is where the royal family worship whenever they are in residence at Sandringham.

After witnessing so much splendour and opulence, we came crashing back down to reality as we made the short drive across the estate to arrive back at our humble caravan park for our last night in Norfolk.

Before our departure this morning, we need to give the van a mini-overhaul as we will be staying at a site 'without facilities' tonight. I get stuck into the usual tidying-up and washing-up routine, and attempt to remove all the grass, mud and fluff from the man-made fibre carpets in the main living area. Meanwhile, Laurie 'enthusiastically' carries out his chores of emptying the chemical loo, draining the waste tank, changing the gas bottles and filling up with fresh water. It's a continual round of activity and excitement when you live in one of these units for any length of time!

Finally vacating the camp site just after 9.30 a.m., we again set out to visit Walsingham Priory before driving on to Norwich. Luck was with us this morning — the sun was shining, the birds were in full song and the priory gates were open. We walked through the shop and out the back door into a wonderful, woodland setting. There was a sea of bluebells giving off their

A soft pastel capturing the beauty of a flower-decked column at Castle Acre Priory

heady smell, a sprinkling of resilient, pure white snowdrops, the occasional smattering of golden daffodils and narcissi, and so much more. And rising out of the clearing, is the impressive east end of the Augustinian priory, still resplendent with its knapped flintstone finish after more than eight hundred years. (Almost with a sense of *déjà-vu*, I recalled how similar in appearance this was to the remains of Gisborough Priory in Yorkshire.) Apart from the east wall, the only other medieval building that survives is the gatehouse, and a re-erected Norman archway through to a couple of 'healing' wells. Reading the history of Walsingham, I now understand why the whole village appears to be a living shrine to the Virgin Mary; apparently, following a 'miraculous appearance', it became one of the most celebrated places of pilgrimage in medieval England, with the priory growing to be an important and extremely wealthy house.

Overwhelmed by all the natural beauty of the site, Laurie was spoilt for choice as far as creative photography was concerned. The amazing sense of serenity here induced us to spend more time than we'd anticipated, ambling along the perimeter footpath beside the river and trying to name the abundance of wild flowers and plants around us. But I knew my blissful moments were about to come to an abrupt end when he consulted his watch and reminded me that we should be on our way to Norwich before lunch! However, the proprietors at Walsingham had other ideas, and delayed our departure even further by having inadvertently locked us in the grounds. Several minutes later, after some vigorous arm-waving, calling and door-thumping, a very embarrassed and apologetic member of staff came to our rescue. I've heard of marketing ploys to attract visitors to historical monuments, but this one seemed a bit radical!

Approaching Norwich via its busy ring road, we began looking for a conveniently located supermarket where we could stock up on a few essentials. As the motorhome also needed to be filled with diesel, we thought it very handy when we came across a garage and supermarket adjacent to each other. Laurie attended to the re-fuelling, while I made a short trolley-dash up the appropriate food aisles of the store. Pleased with the fact that I'd shopped, queued and unloaded my items onto the conveyer belt in under fifteen minutes, you can imagine my frustration, and horror, when offering my Switch card in payment, the cashier informed me that it was a 'cash only' supermarket! Muttering a few choice phrases (under my breath, of course), I practically ran back to the 'Swift' and mumbled to Laurie why I had returned empty-handed. I detest shopping at the best of times, but when a straightforward expedition goes awry, I'm afraid I become intolerant and quite unreasonable. Laurie did his best to pacify me, without laughing at my predicament (although, I'm sure he found the situation highly amusing), and we continued our drive around the ring road. In fact, we drove around it several more times in a desperate attempt to find a suitable car park. City parking certainly appears to present genuine problems for motorhome owners.

Having exhausted all our options with the inner City car parks, we drove back over the river and found a large, open car park where we could safely leave the van. What this meant, however, was a good fifteen-minute walk back into the centre, with all sorts of weighty camera equipment hanging round our necks, and slung over our shoulders! By this time I was beginning to feel a bit peckish so, after collecting some cash from the bank, we stopped at a posh-looking sandwich bar to buy some 'man-size' prawn baguettes. Certainly not cheap, but extremely mouthwatering, morish and messy! I sat on a bench in the cathedral precinct finishing my lunch, while Laurie went inside the cathedral to enquire whether he was able to take photographs. He distinctly remembered that one cathedral we visited on a previous occasion had not permitted photography, and for some reason he suspected it was Norwich. However, there was no problem taking photographs here, and we spent a pleasant hour or so uncovering some of the delightful treasures of this great church.

Moving down to the Norfolk/Suffolk border, we pass through the town of Thetford, another important religious centre in the Middle Ages, and on the outskirts find the ruins of the Cluniac priory and the Church of the Canons of the Holy Sepulchre. Heavy rain had again set in for the afternoon so we agreed to make this a short, sharp visit. Hardly any distinguishable features of the original priory church are visible and the site consists mostly of rough flint and rubbled remains. The Prior's Lodging, however, still stands to roof height albeit in its adapted condition following conversion to a domestic property and, later, to gardeners' cottages after the Dissolution.

A short distance away, following the signposts leading us through the front garden of a private house, we came across, quite amazingly, the complete shell of the 14th Century gatehouse.

The other 'priory' of the Holy Sepulchre, a small independent religious order whose canons followed the Augustinian order, is just a quarter of a mile away. Lying sadly in its ruinous condition, this church is the only surviving example in England from the Canons of the Holy Sepulchre.

As we travelled along the main road out of Thetford, through the vast Forest Park, we noticed a sign advertising 'Grimes Graves', and curiosity got the better of us. Heading deeper into the forest, we found a small track which led us to an area of heathland where we were able to park the motorhome. Struggling against the strong winds howling across this exposed site, we made our way up to the little green hut we'd spotted in the distance, which was the visitor centre. We discovered the site was named in Anglo-Saxon times after the hundreds of saucer-shaped hollows on the ground's surface.

Castle Acre Priory — *Norfolk*
*Some exquisite Norman detail found
in the remains of the southwest tower*

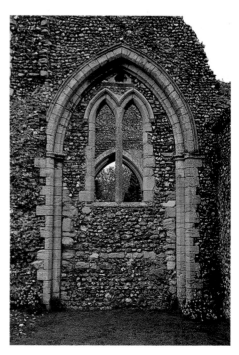

Creake Abbey — *Norfolk*
*A 'filled in' archway
which once led into the south transept*

Walsingham Abbey — *Norfolk*
*The great east end — all that survives of
the priory church — still displays its
eye-catching knapped flintwork*

Thetford Priory — *Norfolk*
*A reset, Romanesque archway
of the prior's lodgings*

When one of these 'hollows' was excavated in the mid-19th Century it was found to be an infilled mine shaft, and subsequently many more shafts were opened. What this represents today is the largest group of Neolithic flint mines in Britain — one remains open for visitors to explore. Something from an entirely unknown historical period, for me at least, and an experience I found fascinating.

Leaving the green 'moon-like' surface for the enjoyment of the sizeable rabbit population, we drove further through the forest until we came across our overnight camp site, the final one on this leg of the tour. On arrival, we thought it such a delightful setting in the heart of the woods with busy squirrels scampering through the branches, wood pigeons calling out to their companions and that wonderful, smell of damp moss and moist, peaty earth. Very relaxing .... then, seemingly out of nowhere, a thunderous roar overhead followed by an almighty backthrust and screeching wheels on tarmac made us realise that there was more to this wooded paradise than we'd first thought! Closer inspection of our whereabouts revealed that directly opposite the camp site was the air base, RAF Mildenhall. Oh well, we'd spent several nights camped almost at the edge of a motorway, other nights in noisy farm fields, and most nights with the continuous sound of rain reverberating against the 'Swift's' coachwork so why should a few throaty planes a couple of hundred feet above us give any cause for concern!

I awoke this morning feeling fidgetty and strangely unsettled. On the one hand I am looking forward to going back home for a few days yet, on the other, having finally adjusted to our new lifestyle, I'd like to keep the momentum going. My biggest fear is that after a few days of home comforts, I will find it extremely difficult to pack up the van and start all over again for another month away. Laurie, however, has two very good reasons for feeling more enthusiastic about our return home. He hasn't seen his children, Mark and Emma, since we started the tour and is looking forward to spending a couple of days just being Dad, forgetting the pressures of being a Project Manager and amateur photographer temporarily.

Anyway, I am quickly reminded that there's a hundred-and-one tasks that need attending to before we set off to Ely, to complete our research exercise on the cathedral.

The journey was relatively hassle-free, and we parked the 'Swift' easily enough in a conveniently located car park. Ely Cathedral dominates the surrounding landscape and is known as "The Ship of the Fens". Its unusual octagonal, Gothic architecture makes it strikingly different from all other English cathedrals. Ely Cathedral's close association with Oliver Cromwell, whose house is situated within a few hundred yards of the west front, appears to have prevented the usual desecration and vandalism at the hands of the Puritans

Norwich Cathedral — *Norfolk*
One of the painted heraldic shields displayed in the cloisters

Ely Cathedral — *Cambridgeshire*
A section of the fabulous painted ceiling in the nave

F

in the aftermath of the English Civil War. It was a belief of the Puritans that churches should remain plain and austere, and it became common practice to destroy stained glass windows, ornate chapels and decoration. One of the cathedrals that suffered most was Lichfield.

Being a very ancient, but small, City, we decided to have a stroll through the streets and found many instances where original monastic buildings still survive in the 20th Century shops and houses of today. One lovely example that we discovered was a teashop, with an art gallery in the basement which was, in fact, the vaulted undercroft of one of these monastic outbuildings.

We finally departed Ely and commenced the long drive back to Camberley in Surrey, where we had arranged a stopover with Laurie's parents. This gave us the opportunity to relax a while, discuss the trip so far, and to view some of the many photographs that Laurie had been sending back for his dad to have developed.

The following morning, having given the 'Swift' a thorough clean and overhaul on their driveway, we then tackled the final part of the journey home around the M25. An hour and fifteen minutes later we turned into our street with very mixed emotions. Glad to have achieved all our aims (bar Binham Priory) despite some of the worst weather on record, but anxious that our enthusiasm would continue to provide us with the motivation to complete the next stages of the tour after a comfortable weekend in our home surroundings.

Walsingham Abbey — *Norfolk*
Crisp, white snowdrops on the bank of the River Stiffkey
with the old Pack Horse Bridge in the background

Chapter Two

Well, it's Monday morning already — the weekend has simply vanished. The kids were delivered safely back to Mum last night, the washing and ironing is up-to-date, the food provisions for the first week have been bought, and all that remains to do now is collect the 'Swift' from its secure parking area and load up again for the next leg of the tour. By 10.30, we were pulling away from the house and beginning our journey in a northwesterly direction to Oxford, the weather looking cloudy and changeable.

Fortunately, the drive itself was uneventful but within a mile of the City the volume of traffic became horrendous. Making matters worse was the complete lack of signs for routes, car parking or the cathedral, which was our primary reason for stopping at Oxford. Eventually we found a suitable parking place (albeit some considerable distance from the cathedral) and set off towards the university grounds where, we were informed, we would find the Christ Church Cathedral. This is one of the few cathedrals that demand an entrance fee, whereas the majority suggest a 'voluntary' donation. Set in its university environment, the cathedral felt somehow estranged from community life and the atmosphere resembled that of a museum rather than a living church.

As well as being one of the oldest buildings in Oxford, it is also the only church in the world to be both a cathedral and a college chapel. Concluding our brief visit with a walk in the courtyard, we felt the first few drops of rain and decided to make our way back to the 'Swift' as quickly as possible. Two or three hundred yards down the street and the heavens opened on us. As we sheltered in a disused shop doorway, we watched the hailstones bouncing a good twelve inches off the pavement, and the surface water running off the streets like a river that had burst its banks. Although the day was cloudy, this was such a freak cloudburst that many people had been caught unexpectedly without coats or umbrellas and there was now a steady procession of dripping, bedraggled bodies scurrying along looking for cover. Looking dejectedly at each other, we felt we'd been thrown back into this trip at the deep (and very wet) end!

Deciding this was quite enough for the first day, we left a rain-sodden Oxford and drove up to Woodstock, where we would be staying overnight on the Blenheim Estate. After an early dinner, the evening brightened up and we walked into the nearby village of Bladon, famous as Churchill's burial place. This gave us the welcome opportunity of some fresh air and exercise (not to mention a quick bevvy in the local pub), and gave Laurie the chance to enjoy his pipe. Relaxed and drowsy by the time we returned to the camp site, we organised our 'snug' and looked forward to a still, silent night.

It's Tuesday, it's sunny, it's warm-ish, and it will be Laurie's first visit to

Blenheim Palace, home of the Dukes of Marlborough since the middle of the 17th Century. A spectacular house, and magnificent grounds showing many features designed by Capability Brown, including the Grand Cascade. We spent several hours indulging ourselves in the richness and beauty of this palace before making our way back to the 'Swift' to consume our customary lunch in the car park. Refreshed and replete, we continued our journey northwards with a lively debate on the topic of "motorways versus other roads". As the driver for today, Laurie won — we were taking the motorway route!

The quicker, but less scenic, M40/M42 did get us to Lichfield for late afternoon, enabling us to visit the cathedral for an hour. I was very impressed with this small, quiet City that boasted a glorious Gothic cathedral, built about 800 years ago. With an amazingly blue sky, and such a picturesque setting, several shots of the lavish, external architecture were an absolute 'must' for Laurie. Inside Lichfield Cathedral was equally as splendid, and I spent my time marvelling at its ancient treasures, while Laurie completed the serious business of capturing them on camera.

Leaving the City behind us, we now had a short drive to find a caravan park at Cannock Chase, near Rugeley, where we would be staying for the next two nights. As the urban landscape slowly faded into wild heathland, the bland tones of housing and industry gave way to vast blankets of bright yellow rape, as fields all around displayed their abundant crops. We located the large camp site in a forest clearing, just off the main route, and were pleasantly surprised at the overall spaciousness. Our limited experience of commercial sites until this time, showed that the bigger the site, the more vans they tried to cram onto it. Here, however, the majority of units were static, and currently unoccupied, giving us the freedom to choose a lovely spot close to the woodland area where we could watch the wild deer roaming. Unfortunately, we weren't able to explore further that evening because the weather, once again, turned very damp and dreary.

Our only 'real work' commitment today was investigating the Cistercian abbey at Croxden and, with this in mind, we had a much more leisurely start to the day and didn't leave the site until gone ten o'clock. The drive looked straightforward enough as shown on our map, but as we neared Alton Towers we became hopelessly lost in the maze of narrow lanes which appeared to be taking us in ever-decreasing circles around the village. Just when it seemed that we were within 'spitting' distance of the abbey, another minor road would lead us away again until, suddenly, there it was on either side of the lane. The ruins of the church, diagonally split by the road, and other building excavations are intermingled with farm buildings and implements in this peaceful, rural setting, and a surviving wall of the monks' frater provides a useful backdrop to a, now disused, tennis court.

Lichfield Cathedral — *Staffordshire*
One of the many treasures to be found inside, is this magnificent
Victorian choirscreen in fine metal

Lichfield Cathedral — *Staffordshire*
*The ostensibly 'Gothic' west front
of this beautiful cathedral*

Croxden Abbey — *Staffordshire*
*A stately beech tree and the west end
framed by a ruined arch in the east range*

Close to the boundary on one side of the road, an austere west front with three long, single lancets dominates the site, along with a huge sycamore growing in the nave in front of the south aisle wall. Here and there are glimpses of mosaic tiled flooring, and many examples of superb arched doorways in beautiful red sandstone amongst the remains of the claustral buildings. Crossing over the road, there is fragmented evidence of what would have been a wonderful east end consisting of five circular chapels, called a 'chevet'. It was extremely difficult to imagine that, less than two miles away from this undisturbed masterpiece of medieval, monastic history, a throbbing mass were experiencing the 'hurdy-gurdy', 'thrills and spills' of a 20th Century feat of engineering at the Alton Towers Theme Park. Each to their own, but I'm definitely with the monks!

Finding our way back to the main road was much easier, and once there we followed the signs for Uttoxeter — yet another town associated with horse racing. By my reckoning this is the ninth race course that we have passed — I wonder how many there are, and what percentage we will have seen before the end of our tour? A few miles to the east of Uttoxeter, we come across the vast Jacobean manor house known as Sudbury Hall. Being members of the National Trust — and eager to flash this year's membership card in a few places — we pull into the car park and take a look. After a tour of the house with its richly carved plasterwork and its fabulous ceilings, I retired to the garden and sat on a conveniently located bench in front of the lake to grab some of that rare commodity; sun!

We were enjoying such a positive day that we decided to fit one more visit in before returning to the site for the evening. Travelling down the A515 towards Lichfield, and then down Watling Street, we came to Wall (Letocetum), where there is a fine example of an excavated Roman posting station with its elaborate baths complex and mansio. The site is quite sizeable, and steeply terraced, and at the end of a long day, with weary legs and feet beginning to feel as heavy as those of the Roman Army, we tramped back to the motorhome.

Parked back at Cannock Chase, we ate a good dinner, drank a bottle of wine and slept the 'sleep of the innocent' as we dreamt about miles of driving, hours of fresh air and exercise, and centuries of colourful history. Where's the motivation to work in London?

It's the last day of April and, so far, we have had only one day entirely free of rain — very disappointing when we remember last year's gloriously warm spring. This morning has begun dry, so we are making an early start to try and beat the usual weather pattern of 'dry starts, wet endings' or vice versa. We are leaving Staffordshire and heading westwards into Shropshire for a couple of days, our first stop being on the outskirts of Shrewsbury.

Surrounded by farmland, we approach the ruinous Haughmond Abbey, originally thought to have begun life as an Augustinian priory but later gained the status of an abbey following wealthy endowments. From the extensive remains, much of them unrecognisable as monastic buildings due to major conversion works in the late 15th Century, it was evident that the abbey was certainly prosperous in its day. The church was demolished but the richly decorated Norman arches of the chapterhouse have survived amazingly well, and a good deal of the Abbot's Hall and lodgings can be seen in their altered state. Staring at us through a doorway in the northwest corner of the cloister, a stern, black cow dared us to approach her inquisitive black and white calf, who seemed momentarily intrigued by two perfectly well-adjusted humans showing so much interest in these deserted old ruins! Youngsters, eh, what do they know?

Walking the site was becoming a little uncomfortable as it had been besieged by an invasion of really nasty black flies which insisted on buzzing around at head height and the prospect of them in my eyes, ears, mouth or up my nose, was not one I relished.

Concluding our visit somewhat abruptly because of these tiresome insects, we discussed our views on Haughmond and were surprised at how they differed. Laurie was really enthusiastic about the site, and the photographic angles it presented, whereas I didn't find it that inspiring. In part, this was due to the drastic conversions which completely overshadowed the monastery, and the demolition of the abbey church. For me, if there is no church there is no heart to the abbey, and much of the atmosphere is lost. Notwithstanding my personal observations, Haughmond is still well worth finding.

From here we travelled back in an easterly direction to locate the Augustinian abbey of Lilleshall. Finding the abbey was not difficult, but gaining access was quite another matter as the only visible entrance was along a farm track, currently barred by a padlocked metal gate. As English Heritage are the guardians of this site, we consulted their latest handbook only to discover that the opening times had changed since last year, and were now restricted to weekends only. Looking at our schedule, we wondered if it would be possible to rearrange a visit to Lilleshall Abbey on a Saturday or Sunday in the next two weeks. This proved to be out of the question, and we felt a little annoyed with ourselves for having overlooked such a basic step in the planning as checking the opening times in the updated yearly handbook. We were about to move on when a tractor pulled up in front of the gates, and my determination clicked into overdrive, bringing out those irresistible feminine traits. With an appealing smile, a plea of simple ignorance and a bit of a hard-luck story, I enquired if it would be possible for us to leave the motorhome parked down the road and walk up the lane to the ruins. The farmer, however, was more than happy to leave the gate open, allowing us to drive up to the site for a

Haughmond Abbey — *Shropshire*
*The infirmary and abbot's hall in the southern cloister,
shows a surprisingly 'unmonastic' oriel window*

Lillieshall Abbey — *Shropshire*
*Local Triassic red sandstone gives the west front
of this abbey its sturdy, almost timeless, appearance*

closer look at the abbey. Very fortuitous.

What majestic ruins they were — standing to almost full height, built of a deep red sandstone, and with plenty of elaborate Romanesque detail still very much in evidence. Looking through the west front door of the church up the long, bare nave, the east window provided a perfect frame for a beautiful display of variegated tree foliage. It was such a lovely wooded setting, the warm brick tones of the abbey completely harmonising with the natural growth surrounding it, and the lush, green lawns carpeting the length of the open nave. We were able to get an interesting overview of much of the site by ascending the spiral stairs along the north wall of the church. (From reading the guidebook at a later date — that we were able to purchase at Boscobel House — we learned that only a partial excavation of this site has ever taken place due to a mining operation by the National Coal Board which caused considerable subsidence to the area.) However, what there is to be seen is both extensive and evocative — but only on Saturday and Sunday afternoons!

To ensure that we didn't get into the habit of 'slacking' on one of our working days, we managed to fit another priory on today's agenda. Driving back to the Staffordshire border, we were looking for White Ladies Priory but once again were foiled in our attempts to get the 'Swift' past a width restriction on the approach road. We noticed at the road junction another English Heritage property — Boscobel House — and swung the van into the large car park to read up on the house. Finding there was an historical connection between the house and the priory was a bonus, and we decided to take a tour of the house before venturing the mile or so down the lane to the priory. But first, with the prospect of a cold, damp walk later, I thought a good, hot curry would go down rather well and set about preparing the 'car park special' for today. It is quite amusing when other visitors in the car park become aware of the cooking smells drifting through the open windows of the motorhome. Their noses start to twitch, and their mouths almost visibly water, as they look around for the source of these tantalising aromas, and yet never find that inviting cafeteria! With a wicked smugness, we heartily tuck into our delicious 'home-cooked' meal, leaving our drooling onlookers to consume the contents of their pre-packed lunch boxes!

The tour of Boscobel House was extremely interesting and we learned that this was where King Charles II sheltered to avoid capture in 1651, and where he hid in the famous oak tree. He also took refuge at White Ladies House. The house no longer exists but the fragmented remains of the medieval church still occupies the site. White Ladies Priory was a small house of Augustinian nuns whose known history appears uneventful. Hidden in the woods, about a mile and a half down the lane, this almost forgotten simple priory church looks a sorry sight indeed, with only a few gravestones propped against the north walls of the church to remind us of its past life. Having lugged a load of heavy camera equipment around for the past few days was beginning to have an adverse effect on Laurie's back. His posture has always left a lot to be desired and it was not unusual for him to suffer with backache. Unfortunately, we had to face a long, uphill trek back to the 'Swift', carrying the normal quota of weighty gear, and battling against the wind and rain. I carried as much of the load as I could manage and we took a slow and uncomfortable walk back to the car park, thinking all the while of that refreshing pot of tea just minutes away.

A short sprint up the A41 brought us to Newport in Shropshire, where we were staying at a CL (a small, privately-owned site, certificated by the Caravan Club for members only). Even though it was in the middle of a town, situated behind a pub, it was a delightfully peaceful site at the back of a small cul-de-sac of pretty bungalows. Once we'd 'hooked up' for the evening, we had a quick wash and brush up and walked into the town's small hotel for a welcome drink, (and for Laurie, his evening reward of a smooth, cool bowlful of Black Cavendish), whilst we discussed the day's work and its associated problems.

Refreshed and revitalised, following a night of deep, dreamless sleep, we were up early this morning, and raring to go. I was looking forward to returning to a couple of places where we'd been able to stop only briefly on a previous occasion, over two and a half years ago, and also to discovering the Ironbridge Gorge Museum, which we had decided to visit whilst in the locality.

First stop then was Buildwas Abbey, nestling in the glorious Severn Valley, a modest Cistercian house that remained largely unaltered during its working life. The dominant features are, undoubtedly, the thick, bold Norman columns standing defiantly along the length of the nave, very severe but very imposing.

The church was constructed without a north aisle because of the lie of the land, and the cloister on a much lower level. Almost complete, the chapterhouse displays some fine rib vaulting and decorated capitals, as well as an area of re-laid mosaic floor tiles. Stepping out of the chapterhouse, we encountered a couple of young constables concealing themselves beside the wall of the sacristy. Slightly alarmed by a 'police presence', I stood and surveyed the site for an apparent misdemeanour, and was intrigued to see a 'drunk' lying on a bench beside the cloister garth with a group of young children apparently taunting him. Soon, all was revealed as the lady constable blew her whistle and assembled the 'players' — it was an "Awareness for children" activity week, giving them advice on the nasty things they may come up against in the real (sometimes, ugly) world we live in. They thought it was great fun, however, and we found it equally amusing.

Lillieshall Abbey — *Shropshire*
A pretty display of wild flowers and mosses spreading across a Romanesque capital

White Ladies Priory — *Shropshire*
Some lovely detail on a remaining doorway

Wenlock Priory — *Shropshire*
Two beautifully carved figures (apostles) on the decorated lavatorium

Two miles along the road, we came to Ironbridge — so called because of the construction, by Abraham Darby in 1779, of the first cast-iron bridge across the River Severn. Like typical tourists to the area, we walked the bridge and bought our certificate of authenticity from the Toll House, we visited one of the museums, Laurie took the customary photos, we browsed the shops around the market square, and purchased another thimble for 'The Collection'. A very different kind of experience for us after visiting several ruined monasteries but, nonetheless, extremely interesting and enjoyable.

A quick lunch break and we were setting off again, this time to visit the delightful Cluniac priory at Much Wenlock. The motorhome parked safely in its space opposite the site, we crossed the lane and climbed up to see the ruins set in their beautifully maintained grounds. Long before this priory was built, there was a nunnery founded at the site, but all evidence of the early building was completely destroyed with the Danish invasions. Even though the church was rebuilt in the early 13th Century, hardly anything remains except for a section of the south transept, and the nave column bases which give a good idea of the overall length of this substantial church. Apart from the obvious, historical interest, what particularly delights me at Wenlock is the sheer wealth of wild flowers creeping up and over the ancient stones and decorative brickwork. I noticed bluebells, cowslips, daisies, buttercups and delicate wild strawberry plants at ground level, and many varieties of the trailing, creeping flowers sprouting from the crevices of the walls. Walking to the far boundary of the site, we entered the remains of the chapterhouse to see a superb example of blind arcading along the north wall. Looking over to the cloister, a surviving octagonal Lavatorium, depicting some beautifully carved figures, now shares the garden with a group of topiaried trees in animal shapes. I am not sure whether there is any significance attached to the topiary, or whether it is simply a 'fun feature', but it does fill the cloister area rather well. Laurie is taking advantage of the better weather by playing 'filters' and taking a few creative shots of different aspects of the site, and I am sitting on a bench in the nave, in the sun, relaxing and formulating ideas on how to translate into readable text all I see and feel when visiting these abbeys and priories. I'm not sure who got the easier half of this arrangement; he completes his photographic assignments on a daily basis, and that's his contribution 'in the bag'. I, on the other hand, have to make copious notes on each site visited, expand on them, type and retype them several times over as many months, and then try and produce a manuscript of sufficient quality and interest to coax a publisher into a negotiating position!

Before leaving the 'oldy worldy' town, we ventured up the High Street to look at the magnificent black and white Guildhall building, the lovely church next door and many of the quaint shops along the narrow streets. There was also some unfinished business to attend to. On our previous visit to Much Wenlock, we bought a set of unusual coffee mugs, sugar bowl and cream jug

Buildwas Abbey — *Shropshire*
The powerful, Norman arches of the nave, seen from the road

Buildwas Abbey — *Shropshire*
The vaulted ceiling of the chapterhouse

at the old pottery but the matching coffee pot was out of stock at that time. We were extremely pleased to find that two different designs were now available, and duly purchased one to complete our set. After a two-and-a-half year wait, our patience has been well rewarded.

Thoroughly enjoying this spell of better weather, we set off on a walk along the Wenlock Edge, a wooded escarpment owned by the National Trust. Although very scenic, it was still extremely boggy underfoot and after a couple of miles we headed back to the 'Swift' for a cup of tea. All in all a busy, but very rewarding, day.

Enthusiasm, excitement and anticipation were pulsing through my body as soon as I awoke this morning. Not only were we about to continue our journey northwards with the prospect of seeing yet more monastic treasures for the first time, but I would finally get to visit the Lake District, a place I'd longed to discover for many years. The only downside, of course, will be the tedious drive up the M6. However, with a cloudless, blue sky above us, and a big yellow sun streaming through the windows of the 'Swift' providing a welcome bit of warmth, we were quickly into the routine maintenance mode and away from the site by 8.15 a.m.

Endless miles of boring tarmac later, and we eventually leave the motorway at Junction 36. All we had to do now was drive right round Morecambe Bay and over to Barrow-in-Furness on the west coast. Great! I'm trying hard not to become impatient but having spent the last month trying to keep dry and warm, and the last three hours simmering slowly in the van, I just wanted to get out and enjoy some of the gorgeous weather. At last, we see the signs directing us to the abbey, and follow the steep, narrow, twisting road down to the bottom of the wooded valley. Our eyes were straining in every direction to catch the first glimpse of this abbey and then, quite suddenly, we come face to face with this massive, dignified ruin built of deep red stone that glowed so fiercely in the midday sun that it gave the impression of being on fire. But, most importantly, it was 12.35, we were both thirsty and hungry, and there was a very inviting pub standing on the perimeter of the abbey grounds.

Having feasted on the 'dish of the day' — a plate of deliciously spicy ribs and salad — and savoured a glass of the smooth, black, velvety liquid, we now felt ready to give Furness Abbey our undivided attention. From its lowly beginning as a small Savigniac house, it grew to be a large, important, and prosperous, Cistercian monastery which is more than evident from the elaborate, intricately carved stonework surviving throughout the ruined church. A rare and decorative sedilia has survived remarkably well at the high altar, and a wonderful piscina remains in the corner of the southernmost chapel. We walked the extensive grounds of this abbey site for more than two hours, savouring the sheer magnificence and skill of the medieval craftsman who had made this a true labour of love. Laurie rolled off endless frames in an effort to capture just some of the beauty and tranquillity of this amazing site.

The early start, the long drive, the pub lunch, and the warm sun, were now beginning to tell on our concentration and energy levels. Wearily dropping to the ground, we propped ourselves against the rugged foundations, beside the latrine canal, and dozed contentedly in the afternoon sunshine for the next hour.

A sudden coolness stirred us from our dreamy slumber; the sun had disappeared, the sky looked heavy and sombre, and a brisk wind was whooshing across the site. Gathering up our belongings from this previously sheltered haven, we began making our way back to the 'Swift'. Laurie then exclaimed that his sunglasses had gone missing, and we retraced our steps to try and find them. Leaving him to take a few more shots of the site in the changed, moody conditions, I continued to search for the glasses. A couple of helpful, local lads on pushbikes volunteered their services, and they were able to cover the vast area much quicker than I could on foot. However, the glasses never did reappear, much to Laurie's dismay, who suffers with very 'light sensitive' eyes — and hay fever! Although he obviously wouldn't be needing them any more today, a new pair would have to be a priority purchase when we next went to town.

Back at the entrance, we stopped to have a brief look around the museum which displayed some of the excavated artefacts from the monastic site. A further disappointment here was that the small shop did not sell any china thimbles of Furness Abbey (in fact, they didn't even have any guidebooks in stock).

Returning to the 'Swift', we had the customary afternoon tea before making our way to Grange-over-Sands, where we would be stopping for the night. Travelling back along the A590 towards the M6, we noticed an English Heritage site, and decided to investigate to break the journey. What we found at the western tip of Lake Windermere was Stott Park Bobbin Mill, a Victorian mill that had been in use until 1971. Luckily the last tour of the day was just about to commence, and we joined the guide who gave us a fascinating (and, sometimes, extremely graphic) insight into the hard and often hazardous lives of the Lake District bobbin makers. Following a demonstration, we collected our souvenir bobbins and left the mill to take the forest bark path, up through the coppice and back to the car park.

I found I was actually now beginning to enjoy a subject I loathed at school — history — and had a real thirst to gain more and more knowledge. If only children could have the opportunity to learn about past lives, skills and

Wenlock Priory — **Shropshire**
A mass of blind arcading survives in the ruins of the chapterhouse

Furness Abbey — **Cumbria**
The incredible detail that survives on this monastic sedilia

Furness Abbey — *Cumbria*
The chapterhouse and the transepts from the southwest of the cloister

memorable events in a more 'hands on' fashion, instead of having to plough through endless reading matter, full of dates and confusing background detail. Certainly I had learned more about our history in the last five weeks than I ever did during my twelve years at school!

In less than half an hour, we had located the lonely farmhouse, handed over our £3 to park the motorhome in a field for the night, and followed the farmer's directions to a clearing beyond the woods. I recalled the description in the site handbook as stating, "the site is part sloping". This grossly understated the challenging incline of the field, and had mentioned nothing about the severe dips and mounds that had to be negotiated to get from one side of the field to the other! Like a trusty scout, Laurie walked ahead of the 'Swift' as I drove in his tracks, in an effort to avoid grounding this three-and-a-half ton, temperamental beast before we reached a reasonably level pitch at the top corner of the field. Quite exciting stuff, which you don't fully appreciate until you've tried handling one of these vehicles.

From our position on this high ridge, we had a distant view of Morecambe Bay and, as Laurie settled into his evening pipe and I relaxed with a bit of fiction, we watched the sun melting slowly into the sea. Maybe this was when the spring weather was about to change.

Unbelievably, this is the third morning in succession where we have awoken to bright, warm, dry conditions and I fully intend to make the most of this better spell of weather. Lake District, here we come! We are going to treat ourselves to a 'mini break' for the next few days and explore this vast area — well, it is the May bank holiday, and everyone deserves a bit of leisure time!

We drove, we walked, we climbed, and, of course, Laurie took over 100 photographs. The weather stayed glorious, the scenery was indescribably spectacular and I longed to remain in this natural, unspoilt paradise forever.

We stayed at a caravan park on the edge of Lake Coniston, which proved ideally central for the road networks to most of the other lakes and attractions in the area. However, there was only one road in and out of the caravan site, which proved extremely 'exciting' on several occasions. Not only did we have to contend with a steady stream of oncoming traffic with the road width varying from narrow to almost single-track in places, but we also had to navigate the steep gradients, the hairpin bends, the wayward tree stumps suddenly appearing and the high sections of drystone walling leaning precariously across the road reducing the width even further. I'm not sure that it would have been a particularly easy journey in the average family car, let alone in a motorhome with not much going for it in the manoeuvrability stakes. I am convinced of one fact, though: the 'A' classification (as in A593) merely indicates 'a road' as opposed to a track! I certainly wouldn't

Lake District — **Cumbria**
Looking down on Buttermere and Crummock Water

Lake District — **Cumbria**
Across the calm and scenic stretch of Rydal Water

have relished tackling this route during the height of the season.

Exhausted, but exhilarated, with our 'Lakes' experience', I realised we now had to get on with some real work, and reluctantly looked to the itinerary to see where we would be heading for next. Firstly, we had to make an unscheduled stop at the 'KwikFit' workshop in Kendal as Laurie was panicking about a nail in the front tyre. Being a mere woman, I couldn't understand what the urgency was — we didn't have a puncture, or a flat tyre, for goodness sake! The KwikFit man reassured him that the nail had broken, penetrating the tyre tread but had not perforated the serious bits and, therefore, would not cause a problem. We continued with our journey to Shap Abbey. Our luck with the weather appears to have been short lived, and the rain is very much in evidence again today, accompanied by a fresh, strong wind. Nevertheless, we still made the mile and a quarter hike down country lanes, and across a farm field, to reach the remote and foreboding site of this small Premonstratensian abbey. Remembering all the abbeys and priories we have visited to date, it has become increasingly apparent that the monks sought out the most inaccessible and bleak places to found their monasteries, and this was certainly no exception. With a backdrop of the Westmoreland hills, the sparse remains of Shap Abbey lie on the bank of the River Lowther adjacent to a working farm, with obvious indications that the cows are allowed to roam free amongst the ruins! We entered the site through the 15th Century west tower, the only building standing to any substantial height, and walked around the foundations of the original 13th Century church, through the cloister and down to the river's edge. The entire complex appears to have been squeezed into a comparatively small area, and looks even more cluttered today with the surrounding farm buildings spreading onto the site. Unfortunately, this was one of those abbeys where inspiration eluded me, and even Laurie was struggling to find a worthwhile shot of some interesting feature amongst these bedraggled ruins. In a final attempt to take at least one panoramic photo of the site, he risked life and limb (not to mention the very expensive camera gear) by scrabbling down the muddy bank and fighting his way through the tall undergrowth on the far side of the river bank.

Battling against a fierce crosswind and the driving, misty rain, we tramped back uphill towards the lane where the van was parked. Our last day in the Lake District certainly provided a dramatic contrast of scenery to the previous few glorious days we had been fortunate enough to experience. Under a heavy grey sky, the fells looked eerie and uninviting with dense low cloud masking their peaks, and as the wind whipped across the expanse of jet black lake, it left a trail of frothy, white meringues floating on the surface of the dark, glistening water. Despite this grim and ghostly image, the lakes retained a special, haunting kind of beauty that I will always remember.

Another disturbed night's sleep due to the constant, heavy rain battering the overhead cab, compounded at regular intervals by giant waves of water being thrown against the van as the wind gusts through the trees and gathers the collecting rain from their leaves. Tiredness, as I am sure most people will appreciate, is an absolute killer for concentration, creativity and just general day-to-day amenability. Taking into consideration the confines of our living accommodation, the fact that we only had each other for company twenty-four hours a day, and the pressure of knowing that we had a restricted period of time in which to complete our project, it never failed to surprise us just how well we coped. With the exception of that frustrating incident at Swaffham, we had experienced no violent intentions towards each other — yet!

Anyway, we have to press on — we've quite a few miles to cover today and a varied theme of visits on the itinerary to accomplish. Our morning will consist of driving up to Carlisle and researching the cathedral, and the castle, and later that day visiting another priory near to Hadrians Wall. Thankfully, the journey was uneventful, albeit slow until we were able to join the M6 at Penrith, where we then made good time into the City. As we drove along the ring road, we easily found the car park adjacent to the huge boundary walls of the castle.

Deciding to visit the cathedral first, we walked through a very colourful, and artistic, subway which took us under the busy main road and brought us out opposite the castle. Carlisle Cathedral, the smallest in England, is beautiful with a noticeable contrast of architectural styles from the Norman austerity to the elaborate, decorated works of the 14th Century, and built of a very fine rose-tinted sandstone. I purchased a guidebook and sat reading the history of this ancient cathedral, while Laurie somewhat half-heartedly tried to take a series of research photos, using the flash unit. In all other cathedrals we had visited, photographers were requested not to use a flash, but no objections were made to the use of a tripod. However, at Carlisle they were adamant that tripods were a Health & Safety risk, and only flash photography was allowed. Laurie was not at all enamoured with this absurd restriction, which he felt would prevent him from taking the quality of photograph that he had hoped for. Understanding little of the technicalities of photography, it was explained to me that the low-light conditions of these vast buildings required a slow shutter speed, which was only possible to obtain with a tripod. Well, we live and learn!

Before leaving the cathedral, we made our way to The Prior's Kitchen for 'coffee and cake' to keep us going until lunch time. Little consolation to Laurie, who was still bewildered and frustrated by the rationale behind the 'flash photography' ruling at Carlisle, but me and my stomach were well satisfied!

Lake District — *Cumbria*
The serenity of Crummock Water

Lake District — **Cumbria**
The spectacular colours of early spring at Rydal Water

Back under the subway, and a couple of hundred yards further along the road, we approached the castle entrance over the bridge. We found a strange mix of buildings contained within the vast curtain wall of Carlisle Castle, ranging from the original four-storey 12th Century keep, to an early 20th Century garrison block within the barracks area. We entered the castle through the old, outer gatehouse, and were immediately faced with a massive parade ground and several military buildings ahead and to our left, and, tucked away in the right-hand corner of the site, were the castle remains. Expecting some huge, citadel type castle, Laurie was quite disappointed with its appearance of a modern barracks. However, the bonus as far as he was concerned, was the fact that he was able to take a decent photograph of the cathedral from the top of the keep.

Leaving the City environment once more for the 'wilder' side of life, we drove along a short stretch of Hadrian's Wall until we saw the signs for Lanercost Priory. In a peaceful, farmland setting, we saw the priory ruins and adjacent car park on our right — and then we noticed the narrow, arched entrance we'had to negotiate to reach that car park. We bravely reassured ourselves that the opening would 'easily' accommodate the dimensions of the 'Swift', but I would jump out and guide the van through — just to be sure! Cautiously, Laurie edged the 'Swift' forward while I confidently beckoned him through proclaiming that "You could get a coach through here". In reality, I visibly judged the clearance available to be sufficient enough for us not to have the overcab sleeping compartment suddenly receiving an 'open top' conversion, and the width restricted to space only for a fag paper to fit comfortably either side!

Having overcome that obstacle with a combination of my confidence and Laurie's driving skills, our next encounter proved much more amusing. As we backed into the parking slot, between a group of hefty, and overly inquisitive, grazing cattle, a notice on the grass caught our attention. It was a serious warning to visitors that the cows were partial to wing mirrors, and no responsibility would be taken for damage caused in this pursuit! I personally couldn't understand the attraction of tough plastic, metal and glass over tender, juicy, green grass, but then I'm no heffer!

Eventually, we reached the entrance to the extensive remains of Lanercost Priory, a once prosperous Augustinian house close to the Scottish border. Similar to what happened at Bolton Abbey, in the mid 18th Century, the nave and north aisle were re-roofed and converted into the parish church which is still used today. The monastic buildings, subsequently altered to provide residential accommodation, appeared stark and lacking in that certain spiritual atmosphere, maybe where they suffered so brutally at the hands of William Wallace and Robert Bruce, or simply as a result of the conversion work. I was impressed, however, with the Cellarium, a huge, vaulted undercroft that would once have supported the canons' dining room above. Laurie thought this would be a good subject for a photo — if only I could drag that heavy, wooden bench seat to one side so it was out of the frame! What a amiable assistant has to do to keep her temperamental 'artiste' happy. Whilst he was happily measuring light conditions, adjusting the tripod and working out correct shutter speed, I was studying some interesting Roman altars propped against the wall, thought to be have come from Birdoswald Camp.

Thankfully, the Lanercost cattle had decided that our particular brand of wing mirror was not suited to their digestive system, and we left the site unscathed, after successfully renegotiating that challenging arched entrance. As we were close to Hadrian's Wall, and the priory had obvious Roman connections, we drove the short distance to visit the camp at Birdoswald. Another first — seeing, and walking on, part of this giant Roman structure that stretches some seventy-three miles from Solway Firth to the Tyne.

After a damp and invigorating walk along The Wall, we now felt we'd covered enough of the historical spectrum for today and left to search for our overnight stopping place. A few miles away, on another remote farm (I'm realising by this time that civilisation in this part of the country consists of isolated smallholdings), we hesitantly parked the 'Swift' on somewhat spongy ground. Even with the farmer's confident guarantee that the ground wouldn't cause us any undue problems, we remained unconvinced about our prospects of being able to pull away in the morning, without assistance, especially if the rain persisted during the night.

Well, no surprises this morning. The rain did not ease, and the less than firm ground we drove across last evening was now nothing short of a quagmire, into which the wheels of our motorhome had steadily sunk. Consequently, we were moving nowhere, except further downwards! Several attempts at raising the farmer from his slumbers proved futile — its obviously pure myth that farmers start work at the crack of dawn — but a charitable fellow 'camper' seeing our predicament, offered to haul us off the field with his four-wheel drive.

We were soon on the A74 heading towards Gretna, a place that had seemed so romantic in the sixties, when I was just a young girl waiting to be whisked away on the wings of love. As this was my first visit to this part of Scotland, and we had been up with the lark this morning, Laurie agreed that we could stop and do the 'touristy bit' at Gretna Green for an hour or so. From the original blacksmith's forge has sprung a well-developed complex of attractions and gift shops to encourage even the most discerning visitor to part with some money and purchase a souvenir from the diverse display at this unique establishment. Actually, it has been very carefully developed and well laid out, and the colourful history behind the infamous wedding ceremonies performed here is fascinating. Having bought a lucky horseshoe and, naturally,

Shap Abbey — *Cumbria*
A rare example of a processional marker in the choir

Shap Abbey — *Cumbria*
*Even by 20th Century standards, the remoteness
and inaccessibility of this medieval abbey is apparent*

Carlisle Cathedral — *Cumbria*
*From the keep at Carlisle Castle, the ancient cathedral
can be seen flanked by modern rooftops*

Lanercost Priory — *Cumbria*
*The substantial remains — with the nave preserved for
use as the parish church — viewed from the northeast corner of the graveyard*

a thimble, we leave to continue with our drive along the coast of the Solway Firth, heading towards Dumfries.

On the outskirts of Dumfries, we cross over the River Nith and take the road running parallel with the river all the way down to Sweetheart Abbey. An inspiring name, chosen by the Cistercian monks for their abbey, in lasting memory of Lady Devorgilla who, upon the death of her husband, had his heart embalmed and placed in a silver casket to be with her always. Upon her own death, Lady Devorgilla was buried, with her husband's heart, in front of the high altar of the abbey church. Although the red sandstone church stands substantially complete, remains of the monastic buildings are little more than foundations since the 'locals' used the site as a stone quarry during the 18th Century. Many fine examples of the Gothic style architecture can be seen in the blind arcading and decorated doorways, and there are some lovely carved heads encircling the central tower, just below the castellations. Some essential restoration work was currently being undertaken, which resulted in plenty of scaffolding about the site, and this provided Laurie and his camera with a real challenge today. Walking past the cloister to find our way out, we noticed a considerable part of the precinct walls still in tact, constructed of massive granite boulders and standing to a height of nearly ten feet in places.

Leaving the 'Swift' in the car park, we walked through the village to visit New Abbey Corn Mill. Although this fully operational mill, driven by a water wheel, was built during the 18th Century, it is thought to be on the site of an earlier grain mill used by the monks. Another little 'extra' to today's agenda, and well worth the walk. I also managed to find the statutory china thimble in a small curio shop we passed on our way back to the car park. How many more will I be able to find before the trip is over? And where will I house them all?

By now the wind was absolutely howling and we didn't so much as walk back to the motorhome, as were blown along the street. I keep telling myself "It is only early May and the weather will get better — soon". We set off for our next location but were soon prompted, by my groaning stomach, to make a stop for an overdue lunch break. A convenient layby at the top a hill was soon spotted, and we pulled over to prepare lunch. While the outside elements gave us frequent reminders of the unsettled weather conditions, I busied myself with the washing, chopping, slicing and stir-frying, while Laurie played 'hi tec exec' on the laptop. Not wanting to voice my thoughts at that time, I remained silently impressed at how 'laid-back' and flexible Laurie has become over the last few days — I am convinced that his 'London attitude' is slowly fading and he is now starting to settle into 'the alternative' lifestyle.

It's mid-afternoon and we've driven about thirty-five miles in really dismal weather, before finding the next Cistercian abbey on our itinerary at

Dundrennan. Unlike other Scottish abbeys we had seen, built from wonderful, warm-toned sandstone, Dundrennan Abbey appears very stark and grey, especially set against the dense, low cloud that has now settled in the valley. Undeterred, we leave the 'Swift' to investigate these haunting ruins, and further our understanding of Scottish history. For those, like us, who have only a sparse knowledge of ecclesiastical matters, the warden at Dundrennan is a historian who relishes the chance to pass on his knowledge to genuinely interested visitors. After a fascinating, fifteen-minute talk and a quick tour of the site, I came away with a much clearer understanding of how things happened in Scotland, in comparison with the Dissolution of the English monasteries. By now, the cold, wet and general tiredness was beginning to set in, and I opted to return to the relative warmth and shelter of the 'Swift' for a comforting cup of tea. Startled by a loud rumble in the air, and feeling a deep vibration throughout the van, I had visions of us experiencing another natural phenomena, as yet unknown in this part of the country — an earthquake! Logically, I knew this couldn't be possible, and confirmation from a passing couple of local visitors that it was no more than the army 'on manoeuvres' at the nearby firing range, made me realise to what extent my tiredness was affecting my rationale. I settled back down with my tea and looked forward to finding our overnight camp site sooner, rather than later.

The camp site, called Three Lochs, hopefully suggested that I would be seeing my first Scottish lochs before the end of today. Across miles of rugged heathland and away from any real civilisation, we found this superbly located site on the edge of Loch Ronald, apparently popular with the fishing fraternity. However, before we could 'pitch' and settle down for the evening, all the necessary maintenance work had to be carried out, as this was now overdue. So we began the chore of emptying, cleaning, and refilling all the water facilities, plus doing two machine loads of washing and numerous 20ps' worth of tumble drying. We were fast learning how to be more economical with our clothing, but during this continual wet and windy weather, it was almost impossible to keep our heavy joggers, jeans and sweatshirts in a wearable condition.

It's Friday and it's looking fine. The sun is peeping above the horizon, the sky is clear, and the warmish air is wafting the unmistakable scent of pine into our nostrils. A dash across the dewy grass for an early shower, back to the 'Swift' for a quick breakfast, and then we're ready to roll once more. With such spectacular scenery all around, it wasn't difficult to find a pleasant route through the forest, where the stumps of felled trees were submerged in a fragrant, purple carpet of bluebells, and several deer were roaming aimlessly in the early morning stillness (until our approach sent them springing back into the depths of the woods). Emerging from the forest, the roads were now banked by large swathes of sunny, yellow gorse. What a shame that we hadn't thought to bring our wine-making equipment: here were masses of

Sweetheart Abbey — **Dumfries & Galloway**
*East end of the abbey church
with its small graveyard in the foreground*

Crossraguel Abbey — **Greater Glasgow**
*A 16th Century dovecot,
the oldest surviving example in Scotland*

H

Dundrennan Abbey — ***Dumfries & Galloway***
The grey stark features of the chapterhouse and the north transept

Glenluce Abbey — ***Dumfries & Galloway***
A 'green man' ceiling boss in the chapterhouse

pollutant-free ingredients for a drinkable, home-made wine just asking to be picked.

Turning onto the main A77, we begin to look out for Crossraguel Abbey, the 13th Century Cluniac monastery in Ayrshire. We didn't have to look too hard — the imposing ruins stand literally at the edge of the main road, which detract somewhat from any image of a 'romantic ruin' but are, nonetheless, very atmospheric. The remarkably substantial remains are a delightful mix of monastic and private, domestic buildings on a site neatly laid to lawn. Plenty of nooks and crannies for me to explore, from the complete chapterhouse, the sacristy with its lovely corbels and bosses, and the barrel vaulted chambers, to the four-storey tower, the 15th Century low walled remains of five small dwellings (thought to have been occupied by retired monks), and a circular dovecot. Naturally, with such varied aspects and interesting features to concentrate the mind (not to mention the unusually good weather), Laurie and the camera were in nonstop operational mode. Following my own energetic explorations of the site, I was content to simply sit in the sunny cloister garth and soak up the atmosphere and tranquillity of Crossraguel, whilst waiting for Laurie to finish his photographic expedition.

Reluctantly moving on from this site, we opt for the coastal route to take us back 'down country' to Glenluce. With the craggy shoreline of the Firth on one side of us, and gentle green hills rising above us on the other side, it was a truly picturesque drive along this deserted road. Knowing we were in close proximity of the site, we looked out for the now familiar 'Historic Scotland' symbol which would direct us to the exact location. Off the main road, and neatly tucked away down a narrow country lane, we saw the sombre remains of Glenluce Abbey, a 12th Century Cistercian monastery. Although its harsh, grey stonework is, perhaps, not as appealing as the warm tones of a sandstone construction, the walls are presently covered in tiny, purple flowers giving the ancient building renewed life and colour. In its haven of serenity, and with nature's growth being allowed to ramble more freely here than at many sites, Glenluce was both inspiring and photogenic; in fact, as I speak Laurie is reloading the camera with another roll of film!

Very little exists of the church, but the square chapterhouse, which was completely rebuilt in early 16th Century, remains beautifully in tact. Inside good examples of medieval tiles have been re-set at the foot of the central pillar, two lovely traceried windows have survived above the abbot's seat, and with finely carved decoration in abundance, the overall effect is very ornate. For something entirely different, there are some rare examples of original clay water pipes that were built by the monks for their unusual water supply system. An interestingly different and memorable visit, even though the ruins are not extensive, they are stirring and evocative.

*A soft pastel enhancing the sunlight streaming through a window
in the sacristy at Crossraguel Abbey*

Unfortunately, that's the last Scottish site scheduled for this trip, so it's a short drive back to "Three Lochs", an early night, and up with the sun (hopefully) tomorrow morning for the next phase. On a very warm Saturday morning, I could think of a hundred and one things I'd rather be doing than hurtling down a monotonous motorway towards Chester in a droning, airless vehicle that was guzzling diesel at an alarming rate. However, with at least 250 miles to cover, and an ETA of midday (before hunger and discomfort became too unbearable), a constant 70mph was an absolute must.

The next couple of days were designated 'rest days' and, in recognition of my birthday on Sunday, we would be parking our mobile home up for the night and staying in a small hotel. Was this luxury or what? (As it happened, our en suite hotel bedroom, although pleasantly decorated and clean, was no more spacious than our 'mobile accommodation', and twice as hot!)

Just missing our target time, we arrived at the hotel at 12.35 and spent the next hour parking and emptying the van of all valuables, checking in to our room, freshening up, and gathering the necessary camera gear, before walking into the City centre. After a four-hour drive, we thought a nice stroll into town would be very relaxing. The reality, however, was that we became hot, tired and incredibly scratchy with each other; there was too much traffic, too many people and the walk seemed far longer because we were having to carry so much weighty equipment. As a result, when we arrived at the cathedral (yes, I know we're not supposed to be working but ......) our irritability exploded into a 'minor tiff' — something to do with seething masses, a service about to begin and not being able to take photographs, and other inconsequential little annoyances.

Oh to hell with it! The next best thing was simply to find a decent pub, enjoy some of the glorious weather, and just chill out for a while. This we successfully managed to do; a lovely 'all day' pub with outdoor tables next to the canal, real beer, and a few lively groups of tourists for amusement! Some three hours (and several bevvies) later, feeling much more in tune with the relaxed, sunny afternoon, holiday mood, we retraced our steps to the cathedral. Still no joy, so we decided we would leave our visit until Sunday lunch time (between the end of morning service and the beginning of evensong).

That evening we ate a fairly average meal, in a hotel restaurant that looked far more grand than the choice of food it presented, partook not too sparingly of the alcoholic beverages on offer, wobbled back to our accommodation, and tried to sleep in the suffocating confines of a 'proper' bedroom. I think this is a fitting occasion to amend the 'sweet dreams' to sweaty dreams!

Sunday, 10th May — my birthday. A large glass of fruit juice, a hearty cooked breakfast and several cups of tea later, and we were raring to go and

Glenluce Abbey — **Dumfries & Galloway**
Fragmented remains viewed from the southwest corner of the cloister

Chester Cathedral — **Cheshire**
The superbly restored colours of the ceiling in the Lady Chapel

explore this beautiful City of Chester while the rest of the world slept peacefully. It was a gorgeous morning, and by 8.30 we'd already walked the first mile of the old City walls and seen not a soul. Interrupted, only briefly, by the ringing tones of the mobile — Mum and Dad wishing me a 'Happy Birthday' — we completed our tour of 'the walls', took some snaps of the old shop fronts in the City centre, and walked through the 'Roman Experience — Deva' before setting out for the third time to visit Chester Cathedral.

Originally a Benedictine abbey, Chester became a cathedral following the Dissolution of the monasteries, and its style and architecture span some nine centuries. Laurie was much happier today, with no services and less people around, the cathedral's interior was far more conducive to his photographic efforts, and he spent the next hour proving that point! I searched out the peacefulness of the cloister garden to glance through the guidebook, and then toured the cathedral to find the salient features I'd read about. I prefer to do this when we visit cathedrals because they are so vast, and cover so many historical and architectural periods, that I try not to miss anything of relevance and importance.

Laurie suddenly became anxious about the length of time we'd left the motorhome parked in some "dodgy side street" — having visions of it being stripped out and jacked up on bricks — so we took a brisk walk back over the river to return to the 'Swift'. All was well, of course! We packed all the equipment back in its respective lockers and cupboards, spent a few minutes consulting the map to find our way out of the City, and checked the details of the camp site we would be heading for. As our original plan had been to 'take it easy' on my birthday, we decided it was now time to do just that; we'd drive to the camp site, park up, have an early evening dinner, drink some wine, and then .... who knows!

The site was easy enough to find, using the enormous cooling towers of Ellesmere Port Power Station as one landmark and the M53 as another. Surprisingly, this caravan club site was extremely busy and we were fortunate to have arrived early in order to have a few pitch options open to us. Chatting with the wardens, we discovered it was a popular, and very convenient, 'stopover' for tourists en route to, or from, Scotland. Now all we had to dream about that night was what Wales had in store for us over the next few days.

As I mentioned, the next four days were to be spent exploring some of the wilder parts of Wales in our search for more remote abbeys. Being completely unknown territory to me, I was hoping for good, clear weather to fully appreciate the 'spectacular scenery' Laurie constantly spoke of from his previous visits over several years.

But alas, it looks like we're back to the damp, drab conditions we've come to know and love! How disappointing it was to be driving over Horseshoe Pass and missing the scenic vistas because of the heavy, low cloud masking the hills and swirling around the valleys. Maybe it would change miraculously as we drop down the side of the mountain into Llangollen where, less than two miles away, we would find Valle Crucis Abbey.

Not even the cheerless weather — or, in fact, the caravan park adjacent — could diminish the beauty of these Cistercian ruins in their magnificent setting in the 'Vale of the Cross', completely surrounded by steep, green hills. Despite there being little remaining of the abbey church and domestic buildings around the cloister, there was a strange sense of 'completeness' amidst the ruins. I think this was probably due to the East Range being entirely roofed and appearing almost 'habitable'. At ground level, there is the sacristy, a book cupboard, and a superbly vaulted chapterhouse, then by ascending the stone steps you can walk the entire length of the monks' dormitory and into the converted Abbot's Hall and chamber. With much of the original 14th & 15th Century construction in evidence, it is an extremely interesting and rare insight to life in a medieval monastery.

For Laurie the outstanding feature was the abbey fishpond beyond the east end of the church, because it provided the perfect medium for a truly evocative photograph of these marvellous ruins, even though the poor weather made it a challenging task.

With vivid memories of this sheltered spot beside the River Dee, and renewed enthusiasm — I felt we'd 'lost our way' a bit with the weekend break — we travelled further westwards to see what other little gems Wales had to offer.

Almost at the tip of the Mawddach estuary, just a couple of miles from Dolgellau, lie the remains of one of the poorest Cistercian houses in Wales. Cymmer Abbey sits in the middle of a working farm where scant evidence of the claustral buildings exist in the conversion work to provide storage and shelter for livestock. The somewhat restored medieval farmhouse and cottage opposite the site entrance are also interesting, the house thought originally to have been the monastic guesthouse. At the entrance gate is a notice asking visitors to knock at the farmhouse before going into the grounds, but we couldn't get a reply and took the chance that it was OK to go in. What remains to be seen is one of the plainest, smallest abbey churches with no transepts. It has since been suggested that this may have been originally planned as the nave of a much larger church that was never built, possibly due to lack of funds. With little else to see, I walked to the south side of the site and sat on the foundation stones of the frater to observe the natural wildlife enjoying these most delightful ruins. Laurie, although equally inspired with the site, was disappointed from a photographic viewpoint as the best perspective was

Valle Crucis Abbey — *Denbighshire*
Seen here nestling in the valley's early-morning mist

facing the north arcade of the church, and this was masked completely by green tarpaulin secured by a series of thick, blue restraining ropes. He'll have to call on those creative skills to produce a different and interesting aspect of Cymmer that depicts its simple beauty in its garden-like location.

As I was driving back along the narrow lane, Laurie referred to the local area map to find a suitable 'resting place' for a couple of hours. The weather was now very pleasant and we decided that, having driven some ninety-five miles and visited two sites today, we deserved some relaxation before finding our overnight camp site. Not far from Dolgellau, we found the wonderful Forest Park at Coed Y Brenin, parked the 'Swift', made a cup of tea and sat on the river bank beside the fast-flowing waters of the Mawddach. I was happily scribbling away at my diary notes (between thinking about what to cook for tonight's dinner, and what clean clothes we had left to wear for tomorrow), and he was puffing contentedly on his faithful "Rhodesian", probably thinking about nothing at all! With some late afternoon drizzle deciding to spoil our forest foray, we drove on to find our 'CL', situated in a large garden overlooking Lake Gwernan. I pitched the motorhome while Laurie went up to the house to complete the necessary financial transaction. Nearly half an hour later he returned — he'd apparently got waylaid by the 'man of the house', himself a computer enthusiast and amateur photographer, who welcomed the opportunity to discuss both subjects with fellow, like-minded souls!

Feeling satisfied and relaxed after a good dinner and a bottle of our home-made elderberry wine, we discussed our plans for tomorrow as we watched the big, glowing sun sinking into the fields opposite.

This morning's dawn chorus consisted of an annnoyingly loud and repetitive cuckoo, and a small group of bleating lambs who, together with the sun's rays streaming through the cab skylight, succeeded in getting us off to an early start. We had decided to go on something of an adventure trail today — from our research on Abbey Cwmhir in mid-Wales, we knew there was hardly anything left to see on site, but five bays from the original nave had been relocated in the mid 16th Century, to a small parish church in Llanidloes. Our intention was to find the church and investigate the nave columns.

Parking the van on the outskirts of the town, we walked around every street in Llanidloes, finding three churches, but not St Idloes. Not wishing to abandon our mission, we asked for help in a second-hand bookshop and were directed to the church, just 400 yards from where we'd first parked! And what a delightful find; not only did we see the arcade columns with their decorated capitals in situ, but also some lovely tracery in the east window, decorative columns around the south door of the church and a beautiful oak, hammer-beamed roof, all believed to have come from the monastery. Feeling pleased with ourselves at having successfully completed this part of the adventure to discover some of Abbey Cwmhir's splendid remains, we now set off to find the site in its secluded valley. In the tiny village, seemingly in the middle of nowhere, it was with some difficulty that we eventually found a space large enough to park the motorhome before we trekked off in search of "the Abbey of the Long Valley". Approaching the site from the public footpath, I couldn't help but recall a snippet of conversation with a friend of ours a few years ago when she said "What do you find so fascinating about looking at piles of old rubble?" Sadly, a fitting comment for Abbey Cwmhir whose fine, unfinished church, boasting a nave of 246 feet in length, lies in a very poor state of destruction following extensive use as the local quarry. In fact, further reading has uncovered that stones from this abbey are scattered throughout mid-Wales and incorporated in seven other churches and three large halls — that must have been quite a feat in the 16th Century! Laurie, determined to find something to photograph, concentrated on the odd column base and fragments of corbel. Once again, he tried for the artistic shot across the wildly overgrown abbey fishpond, hoping to capture a reasonable reflection of the foundation stones.

With the added bonus of fine weather, and our minds focused on these unexpected, remote and little known (to us) treasures that Wales had to offer, we travelled on over the Cambrian Mountains in search of our next discovery. By chance, we passed through Devils Bridge and could not resist a brief stop to walk to the bottom of the gorge. A long, steep and, in many places, fairly treacherous descent along the rugged paths and steps, rewarded us handsomely with some breathtaking views of the waterfalls thundering into the mountain pools below. It was only on the strenuous, uphill climb that our weary legs, and hot, tired feet, reminded us just how far down into the gorge we'd gone! Back at the top, we indulged in an exotic fruit ice cream (and bought one more thimble for that growing collection) before setting off again on the road to Strata Florida.

Again, having driven some distance to this secluded valley, there were only fragmented remains and foundation stones to be seen of this 12th Century Cistercian monastery, and yet there was an undeniable sense of beauty and peace that gave this site great enchantment. To enter the site, we walked through the ornate west doorway of the abbey church with its wonderful Celtic designs, a very well-preserved feature of Strata Florida. Looking up the nave, it was a delight to see so many varieties of tiny, delicate wild flowers filling every crevice between the slate, grey stones of the aisle walls. Then the real reward for me was discovering the large area of medieval decorated tiles that have been re-laid in the south transept chapels, and the faint traces of painted wall plaster. This area has now been roofed to offer some protection from the elements in an effort to preserve the marvellous condition of these ancient finds. All in all, it was close to perfection; the warm afternoon sunshine, the seclusion and peace of the lush valley, and the

Cymer Abbey — *Gwynedd*
*The bright green foliage of a beech tree emphasises
the simplicity and bareness of these ruins*

Elan Valley — *Gwynedd*
As the sun sinks low into the valley, a perfect day draws to a close

haunting qualities of these cold and silent stones. Laurie, too, was taking much time and pleasure in photographing his subject.

Aware that we had to arrive at our camp site before 6.00 p.m., we reluctantly bade a fond farewell to Strata Florida Abbey and drove back to Rhayader, arriving at the small site beside the River Wye with two minutes to spare. With dinner, and the inevitable clearing-up of kitchen debris, out of the way, we walked along the river bank and watched the sun disappearing into the horizon on this balmy spring evening. What a great way to end an enlightening and satisfying day.

Setting off this morning in splendid sunshine, we had a straightforward journey along the A470 to Brecon, where we were going to have a quick look at the small cathedral there. Arriving well before the influx of shoppers, we were able to park in the small car park immediately in front of the cathedral. One disadvantage of being such 'early birds' was that none of the visitor facilities were open, i.e. the Heritage Centre, toilets, café or gift shop. However, we walked through the gap in the massive boundary walls of the old priory and entered the small, bland cathedral. The only remaining evidence of the original medieval priory church is a reredos and a peculiar slab of stone used for lighting.

We had our morning coffee in the motorhome while we waited for the shop to open, in order to purchase the requisite guidebook and, of course, the thimble. Alas, it would appear that visitors to Brecon were not keen thimble-collectors and, therefore, due to no demand, the shop did not supply them. Maybe I should start on teaspoons, or miniature china bells, which seemed to be very popular in most gift shops?

With some skilled manoeuvring of the 'Swift', we managed to exit the cramped parking area which was now bustling with shoppers, and drove down the steep, narrow street, running parallel with the priory boundary wall, until we found the way out of the town and back onto the open country roads.

The next stage of our drive took us across the Brecon Beacons (and through the National Park), and with the stunning mountain scenery and a clear, azure sky, it was a very pleasurable and interesting journey. Just into Carmarthenshire, we found the minor roadways that eventually led us to Talley Abbey. Being almost lunch time, once we'd parked the 'Swift' in the lay-by, I put the spicy sausage casserole in the oven to cook slowly while we went to explore the few remains of this poor Premonstratensian house. The site, considerably lower than the road, is accessed by wooden steps and, as we'd seen from our approach, the imposing central crossing tower, still standing to a height of some eighty-five feet, was the only real evidence that a monastery once existed in this remote, lowland setting. The building material

St Idloes Church
Five bays from the original nave arcade at Abbey Cwmhir

Abbey Cwmhir
Sparse remains of a once glorious abbey gently reflected in the mill pond

appeared to have been a rough stonework, the nave was unfinished and there was little suggestion of any ornate work throughout the abbey remains. Despite its gaunt appearance, it was still fascinating to explore, and the cloister provided a wonderfully sunny spot to sit and wait for lunch to cook. As I read the well-documented history of the abbey in the excellent Cadw guidebook, I tried to visualise the uncomfortable life a monk must have suffered in one of these huge, intimidating establishments with only his faith, his prayers — and his ale — to console him through the long, bleak days of winter.

Leaving Talley, and retracing our drive through the complex network of country lanes, we found ourselves in the vicinity of Pumsaint. Last night, whilst checking on the local area history, I'd remembered reading about some Roman gold mines close by, and thought they might be worth a visit. As we had completed our 'work schedule' for today, we decided that this might provide an interesting afternoon's recreation. The Dolaucothi Gold Mines, set in the heart of a beautiful valley, proved to be a fascinating experience, with over 2000 years' history explained during a 'walking tour', and plenty to see. Moreover, it was an extremely warm afternoon and, having parked at the entrance to a woodland walk, we completed our relaxation by 'going horizontal' in a thick carpet of bluebells. The heady aroma, the gentle breeze, and the sun streaming through the shelter of the giant oak trees, soon persuaded our eyelids to drop and send us into the wonderful 'land of nod'.

Although reluctant to leave our own newly-discovered Eden, it was now gone 6.30 p.m., and time for us to find the field where we would be staying tonight. The early evening had become quite muggy, and once we'd parked the van in the farm field, we walked into the nearest village for a couple of pints at the local pub. In the small, Welsh speaking community, I think we made our presence felt and certainly an hour later, when the heavens opened, the village folk will remember those two English nomads running up the High Street in their T-shirts and shorts like a couple of drowned rats! By the time we reached the 'Swift' the sky was black, the rain torrential, and a raging storm was circling the valley. Just when we thought it was safe to assume that spring had finally arrived ....

Even though we awoke to a gloriously sunny morning, with the volume of rain that fell during the night, we knew beyond doubt that we would be calling on the farmer's assistance to shift us and our 3.5 tons from his field. Now, regrettably, accomplished in the art of 'driving whilst in tow mode', this was a relatively routine procedure, and we were on our way back across the Brecon Beacons before nine o'clock.

Laurie has been particularly looking forward to today's visit to Llantony Priory as, some twenty-five years ago on a family holiday, he can remember

Strata Florida Abbey — *Ceredigion*
The unusual west doorway
proudly displays its Celtic decoration

Strata Florida Abbey — *Ceredigion*
The north aisle arcade of the abbey church with
evidence of masonry between the pillars

being completely enchanted with this ruined monastery. Looking back now, he is convinced that it is these treasured, childhood memories, along with his interest of historical events, that hold the key to his current fascination with medieval abbeys and priories. I am not sure what is going through his mind at this moment, but I actually feel a little anxious on his behalf because on so many occasions the reality of revisiting a cherished place tends to shatter the perfect illusion held onto for so long. However, the weather is unbelievably good and that will certainly be a bonus from a phototgraphic viewpoint.

Turning off the main road, we drive slowly along the miles of twisting, narrow lanes — either the motorhome is getting wider as the trip progresses, or the roads are definitely shrinking — and eventually we stumble across the entrance and car park to the priory — and hotel? He did not recall the hotel conversion (even though evidence suggests it has been in existence for nearly 200 years!) that had been tastefully incorporated into the beautiful priory buildings, but then what twelve-year-old would notice something like that? Despite a momentary alarm, Laurie soon had the camera in constant commission, snapping every angle of this fabulous Augustinian priory in its picturesque valley in the Black Mountains. The ruins have sustained the ravages of time amazingly well, and this surely must be largely due to the thriving business around the hotel. Definitely a case of how commercialism (albeit not entirely welcome from the 'architecturally pleasing' angle) can financially enhance conservation. A feature that was most certainly agreeable was the transformation of the 12th Century undercroft, complete with its original vaulted ceiling, to a delightful cellar bar. Traipsing up the hills behind the priory (to take some 'special effect' shots, from a distance), we had worked up a real thirst, and took advantage of the opportunity to explore the cellar, and sample the traditionally brewed beer at the same time!

We were in no hurry to leave this sun-filled haven and, as we'd parked the 'Swift' next to a large grassy area, we spread out a blanket under a shady tree and relaxed with drinks, books, pipe (him only!), and a few inquisitive flying, buzzy things for good measure. It is during special moments like these that I really envied those monks who never had to suffer the intrusive hustle and bustle of 20th Century life, shut away in their remote and tranquil valleys.

Two hours later, and much refreshed after an unexpected doze, we were ready to leave Wales and face the traffic, shops and people of another city just over the border. This time our journey would take us to Hereford to continue our research on the ancient cathedrals of Great Britain.

We pulled into the large riverside car park just after 4.00 p.m., collected all the necessary gear from the van, and walked across the bridge over the River Wye, back up the High Street to find the cathedral. Basically, a fine Norman construction but with many alterations and additions over a period of some

Cothi Valley

A mass of heady bluebells form a spectacular purple carpet throughout this wooded valley

Llantony Priory

The remoteness of the location emphasised by the mountain backdrop

five hundred years incorporating various architectural styles, Hereford Cathedral now presents an almost timeless ornateness. Apart from the superb decor and exquisite chantry chapels, the cathedral is also noted for exhibiting two of Britain's most important historical treasures, the medieval Mappa Mundi and the impressive Chained Library.

Concluding our visit with a walk around the outside of the cathedral, so that Laurie could take full advantage of the soft, afternoon light for his 'library' photographs, we exchanged our thoughts on Hereford and realised we'd both experienced similar feelings. The cathedral was undoubtedly beautiful, but the town felt hostile and neglected. That may have a lot to do with our natural aversion to cities and we hope the residents of Hereford are not too perturbed by our observations. Now, we needed to find directions to the city's racecourse, where we would be pitching up for the night.

After setting up a temporary washing line next to the motorhome, to enable us to dry off some bulky washing in the strong evening breeze, we enjoyed our spicy chilli con carne dinner at one of the picnic benches overlooking the racecourse. A very salubrious setting for an alfresco meal!

With the groundsmen eager to make full use of this spell of drier weather, we were awoken by tractors and grass cutters just after 7.30 this morning. There was the usual routine of emptying, cleaning and refilling to do today as, for the next two nights, we would be staying at sites without all the facilities, so the enforced early start was actually quite a bonus. The maintenance taken care of, the ablutions completed, and breakfast eaten at a leisurely pace (twenty minutes, instead of the usual ten!), we pulled away from Hereford and drove back to the main road to pick up signs for yet another city.

Probably almost as famous for its cricket ground as its cathedral, Worcester is a delightful place with a wonderful mix of old and new. From the car park there is a very scenic walk beside the River Severn to approach the cathedral, perched majestically on the edge of the river bank. Photographically (so Laurie informs me), it is very difficult to obtain a good angle for external shots, through lack of space and high vantage points, and that is why most professional photographs of the cathedral are taken from the cricket ground. Nonetheless, the interior more than makes up for the deficit. Originally the site of a Benedictine monastery, the cathedral has been extensively restored over its nine centuries of existence with only its impressive Norman crypt revealing parts of Wulfstan's cathedral begun in 1084.

Enthused by the beauty of Worcester Cathedral, and motivated by the prevailing sunny weather, we moved quickly on to our next destination. Travelling into Gloucestershire, we head for the small, but bustling, town of Tewkesbury

Llantony Priory
A picturesque ruin in the heart of the Black Mountains

where the church of the medieval Benedictine abbey is still in use today. On entering the abbey and looking down the nave, the space is dominated by fourteen massive Norman columns giving the impression of an extremely large parish church. During our visit, a young couple were being instructed on the finer points of the wedding ceremony in rehearsal for their 'big day' and looked totally swamped by the internal starkness and enormity of the building. But I am sure this wonderful venue will leave a lasting impression on them, as will their special day. It certainly inspired me, with the superbly decorated ceilings, an ornate chantry chapel, several canopied tombs with intricately carved detail, and some traces of once magnificent medieval wall paintings.

Back outside, the warmth of the day hit us — a sensation similar to that when you step off a plane that's just landed on some tropical island. Maybe that's stretching the imagination a bit, but it had got very warm and we were still plodding around in jog bottoms and sweatshirts! A brief diversion into the town centre to purchase a few 'lightweight' clothes would be a good move here, and to pick up a few groceries to last us through the weekend.

Much more suitably attired in T-shirts and shorts, we leave Tewkesbury and drive into the Cotswold hills to discover the whereabouts of Hailes Abbey, a late monastery of the Cistercian order. About two miles along a deserted country lane, we see the English Heritage sign for the abbey and car park. The first thing we noticed as we were parking the 'Swift', was a small parish church standing at the back corner of the car park. We made a mental note to visit the church after we had looked over the abbey, which was on the opposite side of the road.

In its sunny, exceptionally peaceful setting, Hailes Abbey epitomised the quiet mystique and spiritual environment of a medieval monastic house. Although very little survives above foundation level, the atmosphere breathes through the Cotswold stone, conjuring up vivid images of monks sitting in the cloister recesses reflecting on their simple lives dedicated to God's work. It was that tangible it made me want to whisper, as you do in church, so as not to disturb the hallowed tranquillity of the sacred surroundings. However, the peace was soon disturbed by the caretaker/gardener who was busily mowing the lawns and strimming the wild growth from beneath the many large horse chesnuts on the site.

It was a photographer's dream with so many features, angles, levels and natural beauty, that Laurie gave the impression of a young lad experiencing his first Christmas with so many presents to open, he didn't know where to begin. After a thorough exploration of the site, we sat in the southwest corner of the long nave looking up towards the unusual chevet beyond the presbytery. This must have been a magnificent sight with its five chapels radiating out from a central 'meeting point', giving a sense of communal interaction as well as space for private thought and prayer. Under the shady branches of a giant horse chestnut tree, I sprawled out lazily and let my mind wander to the subject of THE BOOK. So many different ideas were constantly churning over in my head about best to present such a work. Would that aspect be of general interest; would that witty comment be understood by a potential reader; should I mention that incident;dare I use 'strong' language to emphasise that point; and so much more? I realised that this was never going to be an easy task but I do hope the hours and hours of concentration, effort and commitment result in a half-decent read!

Drifting back from my brief reverie in the sunny warmth of this May afternoon, I take a last glance across the enchanting site at Hailes, and can empathise with the local sheep who seem so content to graze in the forgotten life of the cloister. Now back to the church, in the car park, that we noticed earlier.

From the little booklet we bought, written by Lord Sudely (whose family connections with Hailes dates back to the 14th Century), it would appear that the church was in existence about 100 years prior to the abbey being established. It is a delightful Norman church with an interesting history and, for me the most pleasurable find, a profusion of medieval wall paintings. Quite amazing what treasures can be uncovered in these little parish churches.

After a thoroughly enjoyable day, we made our way back towards Gloucester where we had arranged to stay overnight in the grounds of a pub at Andoversford. The Frogmill, looking like a pub with history that required our closer investigation, beckoned us to sample the extensive menu. After some indecision (based mainly on financial considerations), we were persuaded to forego the usual quality cuisine *'a la motorhome'* and treat ourselves to the 'Chef's Special' for Friday night. We were not disappointed. The food was excellent, the atmosphere relaxed and friendly, and the history of this original working mill, believed to have been built over 1000 years ago, was fascinating.

It's the weekend again, and the weather remains fine, which inevitably means that we will encounter lots of people at our chosen venue for today. Better look lively and get on the road as soon as we've eaten breakfast. Our journey doesn't take too long using the main route, and as yet no coaches had arrived before us, which boded well for us to view Tintern Abbey in relative peace.

This is our second visit to the loveliest monastic site in Britain, set deep in a wooded valley beside the River Wye — easy to see why it delighted the 18th Century artists and poets seeking 'romantic ruins'. The first of the Welsh Cistercian houses (and second in the UK after Waverley), Tintern's impressive golden sandstone remains are those of the 'new' church built during late 13th/early 14th Century, and on a much grander scale than the original. Almost complete, apart from the roof structure, the church has so much

Hereford Cathedral
*A surviving wall of the monastic chapterhouse
still stands in the grounds of the cathedral*

Worcester Cathedral
Intricate detail on the capital of a clustered column in the nave

Hailes Abbey — *Gloucestershire*
A sturdy trio of arches that formed part of the cloister arcade

finely carved detail, numerous decorated columns and arches, and many examples of magnificent tracery (especially in the great west window), that it is definitely a case of 'seeing it for yourself' — before I run out of suitably descriptive adjectives!

We've been 'on site' for just over an hour and Laurie is still working patiently on the photographic aspects which are now proving both challenging and frustrating due to several groups of American tourists apparently wishing for a starring role in his 'pictures'. I've just noticed another two coachloads of people arriving, so time to bale out gracefully, I feel, and find a quiet corner somewhere in the grounds to compare notes on the material gathered so far. As much as I appreciate that our historical monuments are for the enjoyment of everyone, I very selfishly find our visits most satisfying when we have the sites to ourselves — there is such an eerie quality about silent, deserted ruins, which is totally lost when hordes of people are swarming noisily across them.

Before driving away from the abbey, we climb up to some higher ground on the opposite side of the road to enable Laurie to take some panoramic views, and then walk back along the river's edge to get some shots of the abbey from an easterly angle. Satisfied that he has sufficient frames — well, I think sixty odd is probably enough — we return to the 'Swift' to plan our afternoon, incorporating the other major event of the day, The Cup Final!

We find a woodland park about three miles 'above' the abbey which, because of its high location, offers a perfect reception on the TV, and is also an ideal spot for lunch. With Laurie cosily settled in front of the screen, beer in one hand and pipe in the other, I venture outside with my book and a rug to find a sunny glade where I can indulge in an hour or more of that rare commodity — sun. Lost in a dreamy world of white-clad monks silently drifting through their vast monastery in some remote and wildly beautiful valley, I was abruptly returned to the 20th Century with the half-time score and cup of tea!

Another day over, and another night parked up in a farmer's field, but this time with the added bonus of some distant views of the Severn Bridge! The early evening was still warm enough for us to sit outside the motorhome, with all our relevant guidebooks, maps, and the indispensable camp site directory, to put the final touches of the itinerary together for Phase III of our trip.

As we watched the sun steadily climb into the sky, we prepared ourselves and the 'Swift' for another reasonably early departure. There was no rush today — it was Sunday, our day of 'rest', and we only had three locations on the agenda!

Arriving shortly after 9.30, we parked easily in the town square at Malmesbury,

Watercolour showing the labyrinth of arches
which make up the internal structure of Tintern Abbey

Tintern Abbey — *Monmouthshire*
The imposing remains of this vast Cistercian abbey

Tintern Abbey — *Monmouthshire*
Looking into the nave through the still magnificent west front

Tintern Abbey — *Monmouthshire*
Pretty flowers sprouting from the base of a delightful traceried window in the nave

and walked past the old Market Cross, through the archway and down the path to arrive at the abbey's exquisitely carved Norman porch. Entering through a modern automatic glass door, we were enthralled with the massive round columns forming a typical Norman nave. However, as Malmesbury Abbey was still in use as the local parish church, there was only a short time to take in the full beauty of this ancient building before the congregation started to arrive for the morning service. We vowed to return, for the full history and, naturally, some photos, and considered how we could schedule in a stop during Phase III. Meanwhile, we wandered around the outside and discovered the cloister garden, before returning via a public footpath running along the south wall of the church.

Time to drive about twenty miles south now to visit the prehistoric stones at Avebury. Knowing nothing about stone circles, with the exception of a visit many moons ago to Stonehenge, I had no preconceived ideas about what to expect, although Laurie did say it would involve a good deal of walking. Although I enjoyed the three-hour walk, taking in West Kennet Avenue, the Long Barrow, Silbury Hill and Avebury Henge circle, and was fascinated by the sheer logistics of prehistoric man dragging these giant boulders around some five and half thousand years ago, I think I was more astonished by the number of visitors the site attracted. However, with the fine weather holding, it made for a very pleasant morning's recreation, albeit a little weird and thought-provoking.

This afternoon we're driving to Lacock, to look at the village and the converted priory, which was given over to The National Trust in 1944. Firstly, we need to find somewhere to have lunch, but we want to put some distance between us and the lively groups of 'pilgrims' still streaming into the busy, dusty and now, nearly full, car park at Avebury.

Alongside the main A4, we pulled into a suitably large lay-by and got down to the important business of cooking lunch. Within the hour we had eaten, washed up and had a cup of tea, before we trundled back along the road to find the little village of Lacock. At this point we began to have second thoughts, as we noticed the throngs of Sunday 'trippers' out for a bit of afternoon relaxation on this beautiful day. But we parked the motorhome in the main car park, a short distance from the main street and the abbey, and joined the procession of walkers. The village itself was an absolute 'chocolate box' painting with many limewashed, half-timbered and stone buildings dating from the early 13th Century. Very pretty, but very intrusive for the residents whose privacy must be constantly invaded by the 'tourist trade'. At the far end of the village was the impressive entrance to Lacock Abbey, much closer in resemblance now to a huge manor house standing in substantial wooded grounds.

Lacock began its life in 1232 as a nunnery for Augustinian canonesses and prospered throughout the Middle Ages, providing boarding, education and shelter for up to twenty-five women at a time. At the Dissolution, the abbey passed into the hands of a builder who, it appeared, retained much of the original monastic construction and set the pattern for its future preservation. I was impressed with the medieval cloisters that have survived, as well as the sacristy and chapterhouse with their vaulted ceilings. The manor house is largely 18th Century with little evidence existing of the original church. Overall, it was an interesting conversion but one that left us unsure as to whether it was the country house or the priory that dominated the present-day aura.

That's another rest day over. We now have to drive over to the outskirts of Bristol to find our base for the next few days. A pretty little caravan club site, tucked out in the middle of the country, and within walking distance of the Chew Valley Lake. After dinner we hiked down the lane, complete with camera, tripod and several accessories, for Laurie to attempt to capture the incredible evening sky with the sun setting over the lake. Feeling totally shattered on our return, it wasn't long before that wonderful drowsiness signalled an early night. Roll on tomorrow, a working day, I don't think I can stand the pace of too many more 'rest' days!

We were both looking forward to this morning, but for totally different reasons. Laurie was feeling excited at the prospect of being able to make a second visit to the SS *Great Britain,* docked at Bristol, and I was eagerly awaiting the arrival of my younger son (who was joining us for a few days), and happy at the thought of visiting an 'old favourite', Wells Cathedral. But that was all later — firstly, we had a research trip to complete at Bristol Cathedral which shouldn't prove too arduous provided we could park the 'Swift' relatively close to the City centre. A few laps around the ring road, and a couple of abortive attempts at gaining entrance to 'unsuitable' parking areas, and we had the van safely (but expensively) parked within a few minutes walk of the cathedral.

In the words of that familiar old tune, "what a difference a day makes". Our previous visit to Bristol was on a wet and gusty November day when I obviously wasn't in the mood to be impressed with the strength and power that this building exudes. Built on the site of the 12th Century Augustinian abbey, the cathedral is a fascinating mix of old and modern, with several areas of the medieval abbey incorporated into the later rebuilding. With almost perfect light conditions, and a lovely sky, Laurie didn't waste any time in taking his library shots outside the cathedral. Inside there was a large contingent of French schoolchildren, but once Laurie had fathomed out whether they were 'doing the tour' in a clockwise or anti-clockwise direction, he could avoid their untimely intrusions on his creative photography.

Bristol Cathedral
A picturesque view of the cathedral set against a perfect blue sky

Wells Cathedral — ***Somerset***
The richly vaulted splendour of the Lady Chapel

Cleeve Abbey — *Somerset*
An external view of the grand 15th Century refectory

Cleeve Abbey — *Somerset*
Part of the original 13th Century refectory tiled pavement

Only 10.30, and that meant plenty of time to satisfy his curiosity about how much more restoration work had been completed on the transatlantic passenger ship, SS *Great Britain*, since our visit nearly two years ago. As I was not particularly interested to go 'aboard' on this occasion, I sat on the quayside with a book and a mug of coffee to enjoy the warm, morning sun. Ten minutes had past when I heard the distinct ringing of the mobile. My son had just arrived in Bristol and required directions as to our current position, where he would join 'the tour', accompanying Laurie on his exploration of the ship.

By lunch time Bristol was done and dusted, my son's car safely parked up at the camp site, and we were all sitting in the village pub, tucking into a hearty lunch and a smooth, cold pint.

Following a somewhat prolonged lunch break, we made our way down to Wells to complete the day's itinerary. The warm weather, the substantial lunch now sitting heavily in our stomachs, and an hour's drive along the tedious road to Wells, all took their toll. We all felt quite lethargic by the time we'd dragged ourselves from the 'Swift', parked on one side of the city, and made the long, uphill, trek to the cathedral at the opposite end of the High Street. So how utterly calming it was, as we entered the building, through the elaborate North Porch, and heard the melodious, soft tones of the Philharmonic Orchestra, accompanied by the harmonious voices of a choir, who were rehearsing for a concert to be held that evening. Naturally, this session had attracted quite an audience and, once again, Laurie needed to apply both his creative, and technical, skills to face the challenge of photographing the various aspects of this marvellous cathedral, minus the public!

I acquainted my son with some of the delights of Wells, including the magnificent chapterhouse, where we sat and chatted for a while in the cool, peaceful oblivion away from the main church. Both the cathedral and the City of Wells have held a special place in my memory since my first visit over twenty-five years ago and, thankfully, little has changed in that time to cloud my impression. It is a lively, but quaint, old City with a splendid and inspiring cathedral, and I look forward to returning again soon.

We took a leisurely route back to the caravan park, had a quick meal, freshened up and then drove down to the far side of the lake where there was a grassed area and picnic site. The 'lads' got rid of their excess energy by kicking around with a football, while I chose to sit and pen a few lines, as I watched the deep, glowing sun setting and spreading its molten colours across the sky as it sunk lower into the lake.

It was very noticeable how much more 'cosy' it seemed last night with three adults in the motorhome — putting it another way, it's essential for all parties

146

to get on well together! By the addition of one extra body, the whole morning routine went surprisingly out of kilter, but eventually we had all breakfasted, showered, dressed and tidied and were ready for Tuesday's hectic schedule.

Our first site involved a lengthy drive to the Somerset/Devon border, close to the Bristol Channel, where we found the 12th Century remains of Cleeve Abbey. Another Cistercian monastery built on the strict and simple lines their ruling imposed, Vallis Florida (as Cleeve was originally known, meaning Vale of Flowers) was founded as a daughter house to Revesby Abbey in Lincolnshire. Although nothing of the abbey church survives, the claustral buildings are virtually complete, and the whole site is extremely impressive. A fine example of the monks' dormitory, as first constructed in the 13th Century, provides a rare and fascinating insight into medieval religious life. Considering Cleeve was utilised as a farm for more than three hundred years, it is remarkable to see the well-preserved condition of some of the excavated artefacts, such as the tiled floor of the original refectory. Then there is a fabulous 15th Century wall painting to be seen covering one entire wall of a small room at the top of the old refectory stairs.

A few hours slips by quite easily in this idyllic location between the Quantocks and Brendon Hills, and with so much to discover, whatever time you allowed yourself, it would never be enough. Laurie has become totally immersed in his photography, and with such obvious dedication to his art, I eagerly await the results of this work, although I can't believe that any pictorial image will ever successfully replicate the timeless beauty of Cleeve Abbey 'in the flesh'.

Locating the next venue provided us with a real challenge, and we were almost at the point of abandoning any hope of finding the abbey, when we noticed a sign for the Priest House and car park. Although this was a National Trust property (and was not the site we'd intended to visit), we pulled into the small orchard car park opposite and immediately saw Muchelney Abbey ahead of us. From our initial glimpse of this ancient Benedictine abbey, it appeared to be no more than a modest dwelling house. Upon further investigation, it proved to be the abbot's lodging and, together with the cloister garth, is all that remains of the former monastery. Excavations were carried out in the late 19th Century to reveal the plan of the abbey church and its claustral buildings but only foundations can be seen today.

Extensive alterations were made to the lodging during its long period of use as a farmhouse, and it is now an interesting combination of a 16th Century domestic-cum-'farmhouse practical' conversion, with strong monastic influence along the remaining south cloister walk.

Having discovered that some of the original medieval tiles from the Lady Chapel of the abbey church had been relaid in the Parish Church of St Peter

Church of St Peter & St Paul   *Somerset*
Some of the original medieval tiles from
Mulcheney Abbey relaid in the local parish church

Mulcheney Abbey — *Somerset*
Lovely detail on the wall of the abbot's lodging in the south range

and St Paul — just stepping distance from the site — we visited that church next. Further reading enlightened us to the fact that this delightful church had been built by the abbots of Muchelney in the early part of the 15th Century.

My internal alarm system has just alerted me to the fact that it was nearly five hours ago since we last ate, and this problem needed urgently addressing. Back in the orchard, I quickly prepared lunch in the mobile 'café' while the lads gathered up chairs, plates and glasses to set outside on this glorious day. Sitting comfortably with our glasses charged, the peace was momentarily shattered with the agitated ringing sound of the phone. There followed a quite surreal scene with Laurie standing in a blossoming orchard in the depths of rural Somerset, surrounded by nine centuries of Christian history, and engaging in a serious business discussion on a 20th Century piece of technology!

Our appetites adequately suppressed, we left Muchelney for the legendary site of Glastonbury Abbey, a few miles north of us. Steeped in mythology and spiritual energy, this has been a religious site for nearly two thousand years, and much of its mysterious charm is still very much 'alive'. Whether you believe in the legends of King Arthur, the existence of the 'underworld', or the tales of Joseph of Arimathea and The Holy Grail, they have such a strong association with Glastonbury that you cannot help but be touched by their influence.

The abbey suffered severely at the Dissolution and vast quantities of the stone was quarried to build the town. Nonetheless, from the surviving, richly decorated sections of the abbey church, it is very easy to imagine the enormity and splendour of this great monastery. In its unusual position at the west end of the church lies the Lady Chapel, amazingly complete and with much of its ornate detail in a recognisable condition. A porch was built in the early 14th Century, called the Galilee, joining the Lady Chapel to the nave, and the vault beneath the Galilee is still used for summer services. Another incredibly well-preserved building is the huge kitchen of the abbot's house, which has been laid out and furnished as it might have been over six hundred years ago. Sadly, only the foundations of the claustral buildings exist, and their layout can clearly be seen rising from the vast areas of lawn across the site. I think the most remarkable thing about Glastonbury is that from so little 'physical' remains, there is so much spiritual magnetism that continues to draw the annual pilgrimages from far and wide.

My son and I were sitting on a bench, set above the high altar looking down the length of the church, exchanging views on the many legends surrounding Glastonbury, and Laurie was busily creating his own legendary pictures, using the mellow tones of the setting sun and the shadows of the stately trees (not to mention a few filters!). Eventually the spell was broken by the distant

Glastonbury Abbey — *Somerset*
*The early 14th Century abbot's kitchen, an indication
of the power and wealth this abbey enjoyed*

Cleeve Abbey — *Somerset*
*The timber roof is an outstanding example
of medieval craftmanship*

church bells chiming six o'clock, and indicating the site was now closing for the day.

So it was back to Chew Valley for the final evening at this quiet and compact camp site. We were all feeling weary from the day's full schedule and were quite happy that evening just to sit around chatting, eating and drinking.

As it is time for the full maintenance routine again this morning, as well as all the usual checks that are carried out on the motorhome before leaving a site, it takes us the best part of two and a half hours before we finally hit the road today. That's not a problem though, as we have only one cathedral to visit for research purposes, and then the rest of the day is free.

We had an easy drive to Exeter, but parking proved to be a bit more problematic, especially as we were looking for two spaces: a sizeable one for the 'Swift' and another space for my son's car. There appeared to be several inner city roads closed for repairs, some car parks 'out of commission' and others of the multistorey variety that simply could not accommodate tall vehicles. Eventually we did find a small, backstreet car park that provided a very 'snug' space for the motorhome and a space adjacent for the car. Fortunately, it also turned out to be only a short walking distance to the cathedral.

This is our second visit to Exeter Cathedral and it is even more ornately decorated than I remember. What I did recall was the sturdy, squat appearance of the building with its broad west front, the short, square Norman towers, and the evenly-spaced flying buttresses along the massive length of the church. We spent about ninety minutes here, sufficient time for my son to make his first exploration of this slightly unusual cathedral, Laurie to take the relevant photographs, and me to reacquaint myself with the many fine treasures to be found inside.

With our work completed for the day, it was time to make a decision about how to spend the remainder of this gorgeous day. After extricating the 'Swift' from the tightest parking space so far encountered, we headed coastwards to find the lovely bay at Sidmouth. A brilliant afternoon was had on the beach with some serious sunbathing on the huge, craggy rocks beside the sea. The lads, being 'all macho' (roughly translated, meaning 'stupid'), challenged each other to a game of volleyball in the icily cold waters of the English Channel. They weren't so full of bravado when they emerged frozen, and complaining bitterly that some parts of their anatomy had apparently gone missing! Anyway, I found it extremely entertaining and had no sympathy for their self-inflicted misery — if they chose to play at being 'men', then they have to suffer the consequences.

Glastonbury Abbey — *Somerset*
Remains of the south transept viewed through an arch of the Lady Chapel

Exeter Cathedral — **Devon**
A superb vista down the nave looking east

By late afternoon the sun was disappearing behind thick cloud and the temperature had dropped considerably, so we left the beach and moved on towards Honiton to find our overnight site. What a pleasant CL this turned out to be. Miles from anywhere, on a vast expanse of farmland and orchard, there were five allotted pitches and all the facilities of a major caravan park, including an indoor swimming pool and a fishing lake. Being the only van tonight, we chose the most level pitch, set up the facilities, and soon had the wok bubbling away with a delicious pork and mushroom stir-fry.

After dinner we explored the whole site, walked round the lake, across the fields, and back via the 'loo block' to check out the showers. By this time it was getting dark but it was such a balmy evening we were loathe to go inside and lock up so we expended our final bit of energy in a game roughly resembling football. With no moon, it was virtually black in the field and the trick was listening for the ball before running to retrieve it. We finally gave that up as a bad idea and retreated back inside the 'Swift' for a 'drinks and Uno' session until we were all too tired to concentrate.

The following day dawned bright and dry and, as it was our last day before returning home briefly, the three of us were going off to Longleat for a day of relaxation and enjoyment. Home to the Marquess of Bath and his family, Longleat is a superb Elizabethan house, much of which can be seen, along with its gardens, and famous safari park. It was a perfect day for seeing all the animals, many of them with their young, and we actually came through the monkey enclosure with a full accessory complement of aerial, two wing mirrors, window wiper blades and wheel trims. However, as evidenced by the array of debris throughout the park, others had not been so fortunate!

Once we'd driven through the animal enclosures, we parked our vehicles in the main car park, from where we could walk to the house, gardens and other attractions. Being well organised, as ever, I put the dinner in the oven before we set off on our explorations, which I had estimated would take us the best part of two hours. We had a wonderful time on the lake, feeding the seals, even though we were besieged by a large party of verbose French schoolchildren (I'm sure they followed us from Bristol Cathedral!). Living on a small island in the middle of the lake were a very unlikely couple — of gorillas — with their own two-up two-down house and SKY TV! Outrageous.

Absolutely timed to perfection, we were now more than ready for the roast dinner that had been slowly cooking in the 'Swift', before venturing out again to challenge the Maze. It is one of the longest and most difficult mazes in the UK, and very nearly got the better of us. But my son found his way to the middle remarkably quickly — I'm sure more by luck than design — and looking extremely smug with himself, directed us through the channels to join him eventually. Finding our way out again proved just as difficult and,

Longleat — *Wiltshire*
An 'expectant' sea lion with his eyes on the next food source

by the time we did, the kiosk selling the certificates stating 'I've completed the Maze', was closed! Oh well, you can't win them all. Our only other disappointment of the day was the prolonged windy conditions which prevented the hot-air balloon flights that we were keen to experience. Nevertheless, we all had a great day, full of interest, variety and pure indulgence. A fitting conclusion to the second stage of this trip, giving us a chance to unwind and forget the frustrations of bad weather, the long and arduous drives between sites and other difficulties 'beyond our control' along the way.

We stayed overnight on the Longleat estate and, after breezing through the morning routine chores, we left the site and headed for home. I felt a bit downhearted at the prospect of returning home this time because we'd had such a good trip. There had been some decent weather, several unexpected 'adventures', and a refreshing element of fun and lightheartedness was noticeable in our working days since my son's arrival. I doubted whether we could recreate this 'high' following a short spell back home, especially after facing the mundane chores of washing, ironing, shopping, cleaning, etc., for the next few days. And Laurie's children! I suppose it's simply a case of getting everything into perspective. However, we still have one more site to visit on our journey home, simply because it would be a sin to pass Stonehenge and not to stop.

Gone are the days when one is free to wander between these giant, prehistoric stones at this World Heritage site, and now we have to be content to admire their awesome presence from a designated footpath some distance from the outer circle of Sarsen Stones. What an unimagineable feat it must have been for early man to have created this wondrous temple out of such massively heavy stones that had to be dragged for miles, shaped and moulded and then, somehow, hauled into their respective positions. I find the whole concept quite astounding, and unbelievable. But the evidence, apparently, speaks for itself.

Chapter Three

Our feet hardly touched the ground over the weekend, and it's time once again to collect and restock the motorhome for the next leg of our tour. During this stage we will take a slightly different approach, inasmuch as it will be a shorter trip (away for only ten days), mainly in Wales, and predominantly with the aim of researching a future project on medieval castles. Although we will not record these investigations in any great detail, they will be given a mention for the sake of continuity of the tour, but hopefully without detracting from our main subject matter.

On this grey, overcast morning, a long drive facing us, and three sites planned for visiting today, I am desperately trying to summon a morsel of enthusiasm to investigate these Welsh castles. Three hours on the road, and still no sign of the weather improving, we catch our first glimpse of Caerphilly Castle, looking dark and hostile under the foreboding sky. Using the threatening storm clouds in a positive way, Laurie was quite hopeful of achieving some moody shots of this huge, sandstone stronghold, set in the middle of a lake. However, I would have preferred making my exploration on a warm, sunny day, taking time to enjoy the lakeside walk around its outer ward. The most distinctive feature of this medieval castle is its leaning tower, which gives the impression of being very unstable. In fact, at the first hint of a strong wind, this great bulk looks set to topple into the lake, but amazingly has remained firmly at this angle for many centuries. I was extremely interested to learn that the gatehouse, built by Gilbert de Clare, was almost identical to the one built by his father at Tonbridge Castle (six miles from where we live in Kent!).

Feeling a little disappointed with my first visit to Caerphilly Castle, I trundled back to the 'Swift' to get warm and dry while Laurie went in search of new trainers, and a fishing licence! Apparently, he caused a scene of mild amusement for the shoe shop assistant, who was quite used to customers walking out in their new purchases and having their old footwear consigned to a carrier bag for taking home. However, she was totally unprepared for the actions of this 'smooth Southerner' who boldly strolled out the shop and, with an almost flambuoyant gesture, deposited his smelly, old trainers in the waste bin opposite, while she was completing the credit card transaction!

Driving further westwards, our next destination was Neath Abbey, first colonized by the Savigniac monks from Normandy in 1130. However, in 1147 all Savigniac houses merged with the Cistercian order, and by the end of the 13th Century, Neath became the richest Cistercian monastery in Wales. It was lunch time when we pulled up outside the gates of the abbey, and raining quite persistently, so we decided to remain in the 'Swift' and have lunch before venturing outside. As the rain eased, out came the camera, tripod, accessories case, wellies and waterproofs, and we set off to explore this sprawling combination of monastic and Tudor mansion ruins. From the extensive remains at Neath, it is possible to visualise the scale and splendour of the abbey church and its claustral buildings during the years up to the Dissolution. There are some fine examples of carved stonework still visible, and a rare stone handrail has survived in the wall above the remains of the night stairs. Considering the demolition and conversion work during its varied history, Neath Abbey still stands as a vivid reminder of the wealth and power of medieval monasticism, even in its humiliating 20th Century environment surrounded by a trading estate!

Less than half an hour's drive away, we come to the last place on today's schedule, Kidwelly Castle. The weather has brightened considerably and the castle, perched high on the banks of the River Gwendraeth, looks extremely 'explorable'. After an exhausting hour or more climbing up and down the towers, walking along the walls, and scrambling around in dimly-lit dungeons, I was ready to find some refreshment and a ten minute rest somewhere. Laurie was still in action with the camera, so I sat patiently on the grassy bank and started to read the guidebook. When we'd first arrived at Kidwelly we noticed the road system was 'one way' only, and the 'way out' was through the old south gate of the town, the dimensions of which looked alarming similar to those of the motorhome! To reassure ourselves that the 'Swift' would clear the medieval arch, we walked down the narrow street for a closer inspection of the potential obstacle. Satisfied that we would probably have a good inch either side to spare, we went back to the van to prepare for this latest challenge! The townsfolk were obviously unused to motorhome travellers passing through, because we had a few bemused onlookers whilst making this tricky manoeuvre, as well as a local shopkeeper who walked nervously in front to guide us expertly through the gate. Although we were more than grateful for his assistance, I am sure he was primarily concerned with the preservation of the archway rather than any mishap to the motorhome.

Absolutely shattered by now, we quickly drove the few miles along the road to our overnight camp site, which turned out to be a welcoming CL run by a family from Laurie's home town of Camberley. That's the second 'local' connection we've encountered within the first eight hours of setting foot on Welsh soil — it really is a shrinking world.

With a relatively easy day in prospect, we take the opportunity of a luxurious 'lie-in' this morning, and do some contingency planning for tomorrow. Nonetheless, by 9.45 a.m., we are leaving to drive around Carmarthen Bay with the aim of visiting Pembroke Castle. I say this with a note of caution only because it is privately owned and we are unsure of the public opening times.

Neath Abbey
Where medieval meets Elizabethan in a stately home conversion

Everything worked out well, however, and we parked the 'Swift' in the large public car park before walking up the steep hill to the castle. Basically a massive round keep, Pembroke Castle was built by William Marshal in the early 1200s and his effigy is located in the Temple Church, London. Yet another coincidence, as Laurie used to walk through the temple each day on his way to work (prior to this trip) and only recently visited the church, noticing this tomb. The strangest feature of the castle was its enormous natural cave underneath the Northern Hall — very eerie!

After a comprehensive investigation of the castle, with Laurie taking many library photos, and me making copious notes, we left the site and walked through the town to buy a few groceries on our way back to the car park. Now we had sufficient provisions for a substantial lunch, I was happy enough to drive the short distance to our next location.

The castle was easy to find but, as usual with this large vehicle, the parking was a bit more interesting. Having driven down a narrow lane, we came to a lay-by with sufficient space for four vehicles and, as one was being vacated, we inched the 'Swift' into the compact bay. Pleased that we'd managed to fit neatly into the available space, we had begun to gather the equipment needed for our work, when some fellow with an attitude problem complained that we were blocking the entrance. I was prepared to argue that fact, but Laurie calmly enquired the whereabouts of a public car park, and we drove off towards the beach to find this designated parking area.

Manorbier Castle, still used today as a private residence, was a grand, fortified manor house built of local limestone in the 12th Century. Its 'claim to fame' was as the birthplace of Gerald of Wales, a renowned author, priest, lecturer and royal adviser, who loved this coastal home. Even 800 years later, it is not difficult to see why, because this picturesque castle, sitting on a headland surrounded by a beautiful stretch of sandy beach, still attracts many visitors. Inside the castle walls is an immaculate lawn, bordered by the most colourful array of flowers and shrubs which do full justice to the medieval stonework. I spent a restful half hour or so just sitting in the warmth of the afternoon sun, soaking up the atmosphere, breathing in the fresh sea air, and delighting in the varied fragrances carried on the breeze from this beautiful garden.

Now we had to contend with an uncomfortably warm drive back through the busy seaside resort of Tenby. With much concentration and careful negotiation, we managed to avoid the swarming families, enjoying an early holiday in the children's half-term break, as they darted between parked vehicles in the narrow streets. What a contrast all this 'hurdy-gurdy' was from the calm and peaceful environment we'd left only ten minutes previously!

Back at the camp site, we had an early dinner and then made use of the 'on site' bar to socialise with the proprietors, who were only too happy of the company, and to recall some memories of their home town.

Today was the one day throughout the whole trip that Laurie could not plan for, simply because we really had no idea what to expect. Without going into a lengthy explanation of the circumstances surrounding Laurie's proposed fishing trip with Bob James, we had arranged to meet him today at 12.00 at a pub in the Wye Valley, not far from Builth Wells. Hence, the fishing licence that was so important to purchase at Caerphilly on Monday. However, a major factor that had been overlooked in the excitement of planning this expedition, was that it fell in the 'closed' season. As soon as Bob arrived, it was apparent that no fishing was going to take place so we settled for the next best thing — a long and companionable lunch in the pub, discussing both his and our own future projects. At the end of this extremely pleasant interlude, Bob invited Laurie to join him on a fishing trip at a convenient date later in the year, and then left us to rejoin his family at their holiday cottage close by. Our first priority was to try and book into a caravan site for that night, not having done so previously as we had been uncertain about where we would end up.

That mission accomplished, and with a good four hours of the day remaining, we decided to drive on a further ten miles to Hay-on-Wye, a town we'd heard about but never visited, and it proved to be both interesting and educational, once we'd managed to find somewhere to park the motorhome. Just our luck to arrive on a day when the town was holding its annual book festival which, with thirty-six book shops in total, attracted visitors from every walk of life from the UK and abroad! We were in our element foraging through endless shelves of material, all categorised by subject matter, in the town's proliferation of second-hand book shops. My favourite 'find' (and one I have referred to many times for its appropriateness to our own tour), was a book simply entitled 'Abbeys of England' by Jane Marshall, in which she describes her three tours of England to visit the old abbeys. Apart from the principal objective of the tour, the circumstances couldn't have been more different from our own. Ms Marshall was apparently a lady of some means, who undertook her journey in a chauffeur-driven Rolls-Royce, and dined and slept at the best hotels available each night. Her chauffeur appeared to double-up as companion, nursemaid and butler, and also prepared their picnic lunches each day. It would appear that she had a wide circle of contacts within the church organisation, and used her 'clout' to gain exceptional access to sites and information on several occasions. All credit to the lady who, in 1958 at the age of eighty-two, covered some 4,700 miles in thirty-nine days and visited a total of 156 abbeys/churches. Although we could see the obvious benefits afforded by the 'luxury' elements of her tour, our own had the advantages of modern technology, a good motorway infrastructure, and readily available publicity and guidebooks to all the sites. An extremely interesting comparison nonetheless.

Content but weary with the day's adventures, we drove to the nearby caravan site at Moorhampton where it was perfect for sitting outside sipping chilled, white wine and reading some of the books we'd purchased that afternoon. Not bad for a completely 'ad lib' day, even though Laurie finds the scenario of not being able to incorporate every event into a complex project plan very difficult to accept!

Up at the crack of dawn this morning — we'd slept well after yesterday's unexpected events, and were now raring to get back into action (well, Laurie and his camera were!).

The day started a bit misty and drizzly but by the time we had arrived in Leominster an hour later, the sky had cleared and the sun was shining through. We stopped here for a brief visit to Leominster Priory, the local parish church built from the original Norman nave and south aisle of the early 12th Century Benedictine priory. In the early morning sunlight, the blush-coloured sandstone of this huge church looks truly beautiful. Inside, the stark and sturdy pillars of the nave are a dominant feature of the Norman architecture in this church that also boasts a fine west doorway. Unsure as to what we might find here, because our reference books made hardly any mention of this priory, we were pleasantly surprised with its excellent state of preservation.

From Leominster we continued our journey northwards to Ludlow to progress with our research work on castles. We arrived in this bustling market town to be confronted with an ever-increasing problem of where to park this not inconsiderable size vehicle. Even driving through the centre of this quaint town was nigh on impossible in the average saloon car, let alone a mobile monster such as ours. It was quite ridiculous to expect these ancient towns to be able to cope with the size and weight of modern day transport, and the councils ought to be considering more 'out of town' park and ride schemes, in an effort to protect what's left of the old buildings and natural environment. Notwithstanding these observations, we completed three circuits of the town and its outskirts before we eventually managed to park the 'Swift' and walk back to Ludlow Castle, which stands at the northern edge of the town. This limestone property, owned by the Earl of Powis, is an impressive ruin set in one corner of a vast outer bailey. A round, Norman chapel with its impressively ornate chancel arch was a most unusual and lovely architectural feature to have survived at Ludlow Castle. This round church was modelled on the Church of the Holy Sepulchre, the finest example of which was built by the Order of Knights Templars and still survives today as the Temple Church in London. This is just the kind of castle I used to love exploring as a child, with loads of stairways, a maze of passages, a few towers and some dingy, damp cellars — a young adventurer's delight.

Having completed a thorough investigation of every nook and cranny — and

Laurie having photographed the castle from every imaginable angle, except from the river — we treated ourselves to a well-deserved cappuccino (and a wonderfully gooey piece of home-made cake) from a coffee shop in the market square. Reluctant to return to the 'Swift' and miss this glorious weather, we walked down to the river and hired a rowing boat. I thought this would be bliss, me reclining at the stern, the sun warming my face, and my man gliding me gently across the water's shimmering surface. No such luck. I was 'asked' to row while he sought out different angles to photograph the castle. Such is life with a workaholic!

We continued our journey along the A49 for about ten miles until we saw the prominent English Heritage signs for Stokesay Castle, and agreed to spend the rest of a wonderful afternoon taking a leisurely look around. Primarily a medieval, fortified manor house, with an outrageously elaborate Jacobean gatehouse, Stokesay is such a fascinating and pretty site. The original, late 13th Century courtyard buildings are still virtually in tact, and internally some medieval decoration exists, including clay floor tiles and fragments of wall painting. A magnificent and rare feature to survive is the solid timber staircase, along with the hammer-beamed roof, both believed to have been constructed at the beginning of the 14th Century. In a beautiful, rural setting overlooked only by a rambling churchyard, Stokesay Castle is a perfect vision of tranquillity, and almost untouched by the ravages of time.

Conscious that it was getting late in the afternoon, we walked back to the car park and were confronted by our 'Swift', and its twin parked next door. While the kettle was boiling for a cup of tea, we sat outside to enjoy the last of the day's sunshine (and to scrutinise the 'other Swift'). A little later the owners returned to their motorhome, and we discovered they were driving home to Southampton, after having spent the last two weeks touring Scotland. Stokesay had provided them with a welcome break, as they had been unfortunate enough to get caught in heavy traffic and hadn't had a chance to pull over for lunch. Following a brief exchange of views on our respective motorhomes, we let them get on their way, and we found the quickest route back across the Welsh border to Rhayader. Our camp site this evening was the one we'd used on our previous trip where we had to book in by 6.00 p.m., and with the network of narrow, winding roads it was going to be 'touch and go' as to whether we would make it in time. We did, and all was well.

This warmer spell of weather makes everything seem a bit easier which, in turn, makes us feel happier, more relaxed, and able to sleep properly. The absence of continual, heavy rain reverberating on the fibreglass roof of our sleeping compartment made a huge difference — an absence we missed like a hole in the head! So, an early start of 6.30 a.m., is no big deal, even though it happens to be a Saturday.

Stokesay Castle — *Shropshire*
An elegant 13th Century fortified manor house with a colourful Jacobean gatehouse

We were travelling up into North Wales and had estimated that we would cover some 170 miles before today was over. Our first port of call was Aberystwyth, to locate the castle ruins. It wasn't too long before we realised that the town council placed far more importance on directing the general public to the retail trading estates than to areas of local heritage — so we gave up trying to find the castle off our own back, and collected some much-needed provisions at Tesco instead!

Upwards and onwards we travelled, reaching our next destination a little before midday. Approaching Harlech via the coastal road, we noticed a small car park with a Portakabin and assumed that this was the only entrance to the castle which we could see towering above us. Having climbed up some 120 steps of varying depth, width and unevenness, we reached the outer ward of Harlech Castle. Through the curtain wall, across the courtyard and into the gatehouse, we then discovered the main entrance, from the town, which would have entailed little climbing and far less exertion. Oh well, now we've come this far we might as well enjoy a pint of something dark, cool and creamy from the hotel bar, situated opposite the castle entrance — just while we get our breath back!

As we sat outside the castle, we could appreciate the full glory of this formidable coastal defence with its distant backdrop of mountains, including Snowdon, to our right and straight ahead the steep fall into Tremadoc Bay. It looked powerful, strong and impregnable even today with over seven hundred years' worth of weathering, wilful destruction and general decay under its belt.

Rested and refreshed, Laurie began 'clicking' in earnest — with such an imposing fortress set against a varied panorama of geographical interest, and the advantage of marvellous weather, it looked like he was going to make short work of his 'reserve' stock of film! After a while, we made the long descent back to the motorhome and set off for our next destination, further round the bay.

Approaching a bridge just before Porthmadog, we were requested to pay a toll by a couple of people sitting at a table in the middle of the road. For the princely sum of 5p we were allowed to continue our journey, passing through the town and along the coast until we reached Criccieth. I was intrigued by this arrangement and could only guess that the road passed over the family's land and they had been granted the right to charge a small fee for allowing public access. Although the toll appeared insignificant expressed as a single amount for one vehicle, a quick calculation revealed that with an average traffic flow of 200 cars an hour — not unrealistic on that particular stretch of road — the family were looking at some £1,600 per week. Quite a lucrative, and not a particularly stressful way of earning a living!

We drove through the little seaside town of Criccieth and down towards the beach where, standing high up on a grassy headland, we saw the castle ruins. Leaving the 'Swift' parked, at a precariously steep angle, in the lay-by below the castle entrance, we hiked up the hill to do our reconnaissance of this site. There isn't too much of the castle left standing, apart from large sections of the curtain wall and the two round towers of the gatehouse, but there are some spectacular views from this promontory. The research work completed for today, we sat on a bench in the sunny, sheltered corner of the southwest tower, Laurie enjoying a long, cool bowlful of Captain Black and me content to bask in the warmth with a good read.

We left Criccieth about 5.30 p.m. to drive back inland to Ffestiniog, where we would be staying at a Caravan Club site for the night. By the time we'd been in the van for an hour, checked in the site, pitched up, and prepared the evening's dinner, we were both feeling pretty warm and parched. Making a joint 'executive decision', we left the dinner to cook and walked across the park to a decent looking pub we'd spotted before entering the caravan site. As we sat outside on this balmy evening, reflecting on the wonderful sites and glorious weather of the past few days, we prayed the fine weather would stay with us for at least another couple of days to enable us to make a trip up Mount Snowdon.

A disappointingly damp and misty start to this Sunday morning — so much for trying to renew my faith and praying for good weather! However, with a quick bit of rescheduling, we deferred our trip to Snowdon until tomorrow, and put three castles on the agenda for today.

By 9.30 a.m., we were walking around the outside of, perhaps, the most famous castle in Wales: Caernarfon. Even the grey, drizzly conditions did nothing to mar the sheer majesty and dominance of this splendid castle perched on the banks of the River Seiont, where it meets the Menai Straits. It was an absolute delight to explore the many towers, to wander along the labyrinth of covered passages and to tread in the steps of ancient guards along the wall walks. An hour and a half later and the rest of the world were beginning to wake up, most of them wanting to invade the castle. Being the earlybirds, we'd 'caught our worm' — Laurie had taken several photos undisturbed by other visitors, and we had explored the site with relative ease. We were now more than happy to depart for fresh climes.

We drove over the Menai Bridge onto the Isle of Anglesey, and along the southeast coast until we arrived at Beaumaris. Catching my first glimpse of the castle, when we passed it en route to the car park, it exactly resembled the original 'fairy-tale' castle as might have been drawn by a child. Small and squat, with symmetrical round towers, and surrounded by a perfectly lovely moat. Extremely romantic, and very photogenic, but lacking the dominance of other Welsh castles. As we approached the entrance kiosk, there was quite a commotion in progress, but a group of 'cooing' onlookers prevented us from seeing the cause of the disturbance. Eventually most people moved away to reveal, on the bank of the moat, a pair of fine adult swans fussing adoringly, and protectively, over their brood of eleven dark, fluffy cygnets who wanted to wander further afield than 'mum and dad' were prepared to allow. Laurie waited patiently to snap them, but they were scurrying back and forth, being chased and shielded by their parents, and not at all interested in posing for the camera!

Complete with guidebook, thimble, and countless photographs, we leave this splendid residential fortress and walk back to the car park to prepare lunch. Whilst the joint and potatoes are roasting in the oven, we wander round the little knick-knack shops in the town. A corner shop, that housed the Museum of Childhood memories, looked just the sort of Aladdin's cave that was worthy of a closer inspection. I immediately spotted a souvenir certificate, printed in 1912 in memory of the crew and passengers of the *Titanic*, and knew Laurie would have to buy a copy to add to his own collection of trivia of ocean liners. Delighted to have found something different to accompany one of his great interests, we went back to the motorhome to fulfil one of our mutual interests — eating!

A satisfying and traditional Sunday roast takes on a whole new dimension when eaten in a 'mobile home' in the middle of a public coach park beside the crashing sea of Conwy Bay! Nonetheless it was most agreeable, and renewed our energy levels sufficiently to press on to our final destination for the day. Driving back over the Menai Bridge and around the other side of Conwy Bay to the picturesque harbour town of Conwy itself, we discovered this enormous, striking castle standing on a rocky outcrop over the river. We spent a fascinating afternoon yomping over Conwy Castle (lots of 'clicking' taking place), followed by an extensive exploration of the medieval town walls. Walking 'the walls' is a great experience, but definitely not for the faint-hearted, as some of the gradients are very steep, the walls quite narrow, and there are no safety rails or built-up sides to the low walkway. Laurie loved it, suffering as he does from a fear of heights!

Completing the circuit of the town walls, we arrived back at the castle and decided to have a look at the suspension bridge at the eastern end of the barbican. As National Trust members, we also managed a quick look in the toll-keeper's house before it closed at 5 p.m. Overcome with a sudden weariness, we dragged ourselves back to the 'Swift' for a refreshing cup of tea before travelling down the A55 to find our overnight CL in some country park.

The site had a strange 'cult' atmosphere about it, the owner appeared slightly

The Menai Bridge
Looking back at the bridge from the Welsh mainland

eccentric, and I experienced that prickly sensation at the back of my neck. Laurie assured me that there was nothing strange about the site, and suggested it was just my imagination working overtime, probably due to tiredness. Settling down for the evening, my uneasiness subsided as I concentrated on the magnificent views of Mount Snowdon nestling into the melting sun and darkening skies. It's not surprising that we felt shattered, both physically and mentally as, for the last nine hours, we literally had not stopped driving, climbing and walking on the one hand, and taking in great chunks of Welsh history on the other. But what a great day it had been.

Not the usual melodious dawn chorus to guide us gently into the new day, but the shrill, monotonous and urgent squawking of a dozen or more greedy ducks brought us swiftly from our state of semiconsciousness. Never mind though, it's Monday, it's not raining and it is definitely clear enough to make our long-awaited visit to Mount Snowdon.

It was only a short drive to Llanberis, where we could park the 'Swift' and board the mountain railway to the summit of Snowdon. Although cramped and uncomfortable in the wooden carriages of this remarkable 'rack and pinion' service up the mountain, the scenery was breath-taking. After a long, slow climb we reached the top, and were thankful to be able to leave the train and stretch our legs for a while. Within fifteen minutes of our arrival at the summit, the sky became dark and threatening, and the cold, low cloud swirled eerily around us obscuring most of the spectacular views that Laurie had been happily photographing on the journey upwards. That's the unpredictability of natural phenomena I suppose, but it certainly didn't spoil the experience for me.

Two and a half hours later, we were back in the 'Swift' and heading in a northeasterly direction to Rhuddlan where we would visit the first castle of the day. By now the rain was absolutely lashing down, and as Laurie fought to keep the motorhome on a fairly even keel along the desolate, snaking, mountain roads full of potholes, I applied my balance and resourcefulness in the kitchen quarters. Time had somehow overtaken us so, in an effort to regain an hour, I was preparing sandwiches 'in transit' to eat as we drove along. I'm not sure what the 'highway' implications of this are, but I certainly would not recommend it without first taking a car-sickness pill!

As we pulled into the car park (which closely resembled a builder's yard) at Rhuddlan Castle, torrential rain prevented us from venturing any further at the moment. While waiting for the cloudburst to pass, we enjoyed a large, fresh pot of tea — our first drink since breakfast time. Between the heavy showers, we managed to make a quick tour of the colourful sandstone ruins, although photographs were not a viable proposition because the entire castle was surrounded by scaffolding. Nevertheless, we conducted our research

Mount Snowdon

*The view down Snowdon from a railway carriage as
the rack-and-pinion train pulls into the summit station*

and bought a guidebook — the pictures would have to be taken at some future date.

Hurrying back to the motorhome before the heavens opened on us, we were at last going to find an abbey — (they'd certainly been a bit sparse on this leg of the trip) located a few miles along the main coast road, in a town called Greenfield. Certainly 'find' turned out to be the appropriate word because the ruins of Basingwerk Abbey were not even mentioned in the signs advertising the Heritage Park. Eventually we stumbled across a large coach park at the lower edge of the park, and walked up through the wooded escarpment until we came to a clearing on our right. Here we found the remains of this Cistercian abbey. Although only fragments of the small abbey church have survived, it is a very pleasant site to investigate, with some detail existing on the arched entrances to the claustral buildings, a few good lancet windows, the odd fireplace, and traces of a staircase. The remnants of an old barn, situated in the southeast corner of the site, suggest that it was used as a farm at some time following the Dissolution. Completing our visit with a short walk to the gift shop, in search of the obligatory thimble, I wondered how many 'would-be' visitors abandoned their search for the abbey or were simply distracted by the other features of the park. A few more clearly marked directions wouldn't go amiss here, because Basingwerk Abbey is definitely worth finding.

Our last scheduled visit for today is only four miles away, in the historic town of Flint. Driving through this urbanized area, with its threatening tower blocks and its industrial premises, the 20th Century appears to have completely overshadowed the strength and charm of the once imposing castle, now sitting alone on the edge of the Dee estuary. The ravages of time are sadly evident throughout this late 13th Century stronghold, with the scars of past demolition work, general neglect, and, more recently, the horrendous defacement of some stonework by the use of modern spray paint. Our exploration of Flint Castle is cut short by the gusting winds and the onset of yet more rain, leaving us feeling cold and weary after another long day. Walking back to where we parked the 'Swift' next to the lifeboat station, we looked across the marshland at the lifeless, sandstone fortress standing defiantly alone, and resigned to facing many more decades of sorrowful decay.

Glad to be ensconced in the relative warmth and protection of the motorhome, and knowing we had only three miles or so to travel to our pre-arranged CL for the night, we set off with the comforting thought of dinner and relaxation only a few minutes away. How wrong can you be? We've been driving around in circles (about twenty-one miles in total) for the last hour or more, and still we are no nearer finding this elusive camp site. On the third time of passing a particular lay-by, we finally conceded, pulled in and consulted our Caravan Club Handbook to arrange an alternative site. Unfortunately, the only club site available, with hardstanding pitches (now a priority because of the prevailing heavy rain) was some thirty miles drive. However, it was in the right direction for our exploits the next day and so we made the journey down to Chirk, arriving just after 7 p.m. Within the hour we were 'hooked up', relaxing in front of the TV with a glass of the dark red alcoholic stuff beside us, and about to get stuck into a delicious curry that had been tantalising our nostrils for the past forty-five minutes. Bliss!

Sleep came easily last night, but we were disturbed in the early hours by heavy rain and gusting winds. At 5.30 a.m., wide awake and feeling chilly, we scrambled down from the 'snug' and put the kettle on for a warming cup of tea. Deciding it was pointless going back to bed, we showered, dressed and breakfasted and, just before 7.30 a.m., left the caravan site to begin our long journey in the driving rain.

We were travelling back down to Monmouthshire with the intention of researching a further four castles and visiting an abbey. Soon after nine o'clock, having driven some 100 miles of undulating, twisting, narrow roads, Laurie suggested we stop in the next lay-by for a much-needed coffee break. As I went from the cab towards the kitchen, I felt an ominous squelching sensation underfoot and, to our utter dismay and disbelief, we discovered the carpets were saturated. We could only summise that the torrential rain this morning had somehow found a weak spot in the van, maybe through an outside locker, and seeped in as we'd been driving along. Needless to say, this caused a temporary despondency and a glimmer of frayed patience as we spent the next forty-five minutes trying to mop up excess water, plug any obvious holes and trace the source of the problem. Finally able to have our coffee and toasted teacakes, we now had to decide what further action was required to remedy this 'minor inconvenience'. While Laurie was still 'simmering', he rang the motorhome supplier to express his sheer frustration with this latest incident which, undoubtedly, was due to their ineffective vehicle check procedure, and demanded a solution. Surely it was more than just bad luck that so many things had proved faulty on a vehicle less than ten months old!

Resuming our journey today, but with the prospect of having to make a detour to Tewkesbury on Thursday to get the 'Swift' looked over, we prayed that the rain would hold off over the next couple of days so as not to exacerbate the current problem. Back in the Brecon Beacons National Park, we spot a signpost for Tretower Court and Castle and presume this to be the first site on our itinerary. We enter the site through a small postern gate and into the main courtyard, around which is built a wonderful medieval manor house. At the back of the house, and across the meadow, is the remains of the castle built some 200 years prior to the manor house. Treading carefully to avoid the excessive amounts of sheep droppings in and around the castle ruins, we inspect the surviving walls and tower of this sandstone fortress. Surrounded now by modern farm buildings, the castle looks so out of place that you could be forgiven for thinking this was a mere folly, built in the grounds of the impressive manor house. Nonetheless, it was an interestingly different type of venue.

Moving swiftly on, we are now looking to visit 'The Three Castles' built in a triangle by the Normans on the borders of England and Wales, shortly after William the Conqueror's triumph at Hastings. About three miles east of Abergavenny, we are directed to the first of the trio, White Castle, via a single track lane. Well, after getting up this morning at 5.30, driving for nearly three hours in heavy rain, and discovering a major leak in the motorhome, we are not going to let such a minor obstacle prevent us from researching this castle! It was worth the nerve-racking ride round the blind corners to discover the lovely moated ruin in the midst of a lush and peaceful valley. Large sections of the curtain wall still survive as protection for the inner ward, and the views from the gatehouse towers are spectacular. Retracing our inward journey to the main road (and with 'everything' crossed to prevent us meeting an oncoming vehicle), we travel about eight miles further on to the delightful village of Skenfrith. Even in its ruinous state, the red sandstone castle beside the River Monnow still manages to dominate the village, otherwise consisting of perhaps twenty houses and the parish church. While walking along the footpath towards the castle entrance, we hear the constant swooshing of fast-running water, and find a weir, and, further upriver, an old mill with its water wheel. Not too much of Skenfrith Castle survives but it is a well-maintained site, very peaceful, and a splendid 'sun trap' should you desire to while away a warm, spring afternoon.

Before leaving the village, we walked along to the beautiful parish church, built at the same time as the castle, and had a peek inside. Typically Norman, consisting of a central nave and side aisles, but with much restoration work carried out over the subsequent four centuries. The unusual tower, believed to have been constructed in 1207, is topped with a dovecote, apparently a common feature of churches in Border towns. This would have provided a storage facility, and doubled as a fortress and a refuge during the many raids by the English.

Meanwhile, back at the 'Swift' my stomach was telling me that lunch time had been and gone, and nothing had been consumed! This was easily rectified with a hearty snack, before setting off again to find the last castle of the day at Grosmont. Only five miles away, this proved the most challenging of the three castles to locate. We found the quaint village with little enough difficulty but parking the 'Swift' and searching for signs to Grosmont Castle seemed an almost impossible task. However, a vehicle eventually pulled away from its parked position next to a huge flint wall in the High Street, and the motorhome was gently persuaded to fit snugly into the vacant space. With the first problem taken care of, all we had to do now was go find the castle. By sheer chance

Basingwerk Abbey — *Flintshire*
Amongst the fragmented ruins these chapterhouse arches have somehow survived

Abbey Dore — *Hereford & Worcs*
East end and transepts of the medieval church now form the parish church

I noticed, on the side wall of a house, a small plaque displaying "ancient monument", just peeping through a mass of overgrown foliage. This lead us up what appeared to be a driveway, with an entrance into the castle grounds about two hundred yards further on. But before reaching the castle walls, our attention was drawn to a prominent warning sign pinned to a huge tree trunk advising us to "Beware of the Bull". Terrific! First they try and cover up the directions to the castle and then, if you pass that test, they try and scare you away with the threat of a bull. I get the impression that someone, somewhere does not feel inclined to share the pleasures of these charming, secluded remains. The sparse indications of a once fine, royal castle did not take long to explore.

Having completed the triangle of castles, we were now ready to pursue our primary objective of visiting an ancient abbey. In less than twenty minutes, we were parking in front of Abbey Dore — the abbey by the stream. The presbytery and transepts of the original Cistercian abbey remain today in use as the parish church, and is all that survives, apart from two nave arcade columns abutted to the west wall on the outside of the church. Much of the interior is the original 12th Century construction but, with major restoration works carried out in the Renaissance style, the abbey's stark Norman architecture is beautifully enhanced. On our way out of the church, we saw a notice about Abbey Dore Court Garden and thought we might end the day with a brief visit, as it had turned out to be such a warm afternoon.

What an unexpected and diverse place, with a fascinating history connecting it loosely to the ancient Cistercian abbey we had just visited. The present owners have turned their plot of some 135 acres into the most delightful gardens featuring a river walk, an orchard, a traditional 'old fashioned' area full of colour and fragrance, a water garden and so much more. There is also a well-stocked tearoom, with some tempting home-made dishes, a gift shop and a Teddy Bear 'gallery'. It is a perfect sanctuary for appreciating the vivid colours and heady aromas of a garden that has been lovingly nurtured over the last twenty years. Definitely a deep sense of being 'at one with nature' for a brief interlude, in a world where it is all too easy to forget these simple pleasures. Well done Charis Ward.

Now we have only a short drive down the A465 towards Abergavenny before we reach Pandy, where we will be staying overnight. There was a thoughtful note in the caravan site handbook about a railway line adjacent to the site, but what they omitted to advise was that the pitches were almost on the track! This was going to be an exciting night.

After a surprisingly good night's sleep — thankfully the trains did not disturb us in the slightest — we awoke to the rhythmic, pitter-patter of rain. We had actually got to the stage of accepting wet weather as the norm, after all it had

Abbey Dore — **Hereford & Worcs**
Exposed remains of the Norman nave columns

Malmesbury Abbey — **Wiltshire**
The austere Norman nave

rained for more or less the whole of April, half of May, and now for the first three days of June. Were we going to get any summer this year?

From the time we left the caravan site, until we reached Raglan an hour later, the rain became heavier and heavier, and we became concerned at how 'the leak' would hold up to these torrential conditions. As soon as we stopped in front of Raglan Castle, we carried out a quick check on all the cloths and towels we'd used to soak up any excess water and 'plug' potential inlets, and were satisfied that the problem was temporarily under control. By the time we were ready to explore the castle, two coaches had deposited their complement of excited schoolchildren at the entrance. Great! During most of our visit we were consciously avoiding areas of the castle where they were noisily swarming over, but 100 children have the uncanny knack of being in every place at once! Between the showers, and the 'little darlings', Laurie did manage to photograph the site quite systematically, while I busily made notes on the most interesting and decorative features. From the extensive remains as seen today, it must have been a spectacular and lavish residence in the 17th Century, surrounded with a pretty moat providing a colourful display of water lillies.

The rain was persisting in trying to spoil the day but we hardly noticed it as we concentrated our minds on finishing our 'castles' research schedule with a drive to Chepstow. It was almost one o'clock as we parked the 'Swift' in front of Chepstow Castle, which meant another gourmet dish from 'Linda's lunch time menu' was about to be served in the car park. Having eaten, washed-up and cleared away, we now waited for the enormous black cloud to pass overhead before setting off to explore this magnificent, Norman castle. Built in the natural lie of the land, on three distinct levels of the cliff face, Chepstow sprawls along the banks of the River Wye on the English/Welsh border. It is such a marvellous castle for the 'surprise element' and warrants a good couple of hours' inspection to do it full justice. When we'd completed our respective labours for documenting our visit from the inside of the castle, we walked across the bridge and viewed this splendid fortress from the other side of the river. I'm sure we will be returning to Chepstow in the not too distant future, as it remains one of our favourites.

That completes our deviation into castles on this trip — and how refreshing and enjoyable it has been — but we have one more abbey to see before we make tracks for home tomorrow. Tonight we had pre-booked to stay at Cirencester, thinking that it would only mean a short drive to Malmsbury in the morning, and then drop onto the M4 to head for home. However, we now have to travel back up to Tewkesbury first thing tomorrow in order to get the 'Swift' inspected for the leak, and any subsequent water damage sustained. Such time wasting and inconvenience is more than mildly irritating when a well-planned schedule with tight deadlines have to be met for the

M

Malmesbury Abbey — *Wiltshire*
Beautifully carved figures of the apostles set above the south porch doorway

successful completion of this project.

Reassessing the schedule and the time available, we decide to squeeze in a visit to Malmsbury Abbey before going back to the caravan site this evening. Having briefly seen the abbey only three weeks ago, Laurie knew exactly what he would be photographing, and I had now read the guidebook pointing out the salient features of this magnificent old church. This little country town is far busier this afternoon than it was on the Sunday morning of our previous visit, and we had to park the motorhome in the main car park, from where we could see the abbey dominating Malmsbury from its hilltop position. As we approached the entrance, we recalled the exquisitely carved porch and, seeing again the craftsmanship and skill of our Norman ancestors, it really brought home to us the enormity of this task. The attention to detail on these superb carvings of the twelve apostles inside the porch, and the several Bible stories depicted in the doorway arches, is almost unbelievable. Stepping inside, it's not only our eyes that are awakened to the delights of this glorious building, but our ears are treated to the harmonious and powerful chords of the organ reverberating throughout the church. The starkness of the typically Norman nave emits atmosphere and beauty from the pure and simple elegance of its bold construction. The Parvise, or Treasury, exhibits four volumes of magnificently illustrated scripture books dating back to 1407, along with many engravings, sketches and paintings of the abbey throughout its history. Outside the church, the remains of the west front and the crossing arch for the tower can be seen, as well as a secluded, relaid cloister garden. Although not massive by monastic standards, this Benedictine abbey surely must have been an impressive sight before the Dissolution.

Malmsbury Abbey certainly has to rank high amongst 'our favourite's list', with its distinctive contrast between completeness and ruins. Words are a poor substitute for appreciating the beautiful image it creates, and quite meaningless for expressing the emotions caused by its haunting atmosphere.

Satisfied that I've covered every aspect of the abbey, and Laurie has managed to photograph the majority of it, we journey on to the caravan site, and hope that tomorrow's unwelcome detour will not prove too onerous.

At least it's a dry start to the day, so already we feel less frustrated about having to drive an additional eighty-five miles before we even begin our homeward journey. Unfortunately, because we do not want to prolong the day and arrive home too late, we get caught up in the early-morning rush-hour traffic and don't arrive in Tewkesbury until just after ten o'clock.

Outlining the recent problems with the 'Swift' (in graphic detail) to the service manager, he promises to undertake a comprehensive investigation, and provide us with a full report when we collect the van in approximately two hours! So our final challenge of this phase seems to be 'how to kill the rest of the morning?'. We have a dislike of towns in general; we do not enjoy 'looking round the shops'; the only place of interest, i.e. the abbey, we'd previously visited; and all we really want to do is go home.

However, our first priority was a coffee shop for an early 'elevenses' and, in pursuit of this objective, we passed a 'real' tea and coffee retailers that caught our attention as a possible stopping place for later. Over a frothy coffee and a slice of passion cake, I thought of a few essentials that we needed to buy before going home, and, not to be outdone, Laurie added in a couple of extravagances! With the boring shopping taken care of, we walked back to Pickwicks, the teashop. Both being 'real tea' freaks, we took great pleasure in sniffing out the forty-odd varieties and comparing the smell, texture and appearance with those of our regular supplier. As well as purchasing half a dozen 'new' teas, we also bought a dozen oriental black tea tins, which I'd been searching for, without success, for over two years. Sometimes even the most unlikely, and unplanned, excursions have their compensations.

Back at the caravan centre, the news wasn't too optimistic. It seemed likely that the van would have to be returned to 'Swift' to be 'stripped down' and fully assessed for leakage and water damage, the necessary repairs undertaken, and then rebuilt — in total, some three or four weeks off the road! Feeling a bit downhearted at the prospect of this major work, we commenced our journey back to Kent, stopping only briefly at the motorway services for a late lunch, before facing the inevitable pleasures of the M25. Home again, briefly.

Watercolour observation of Tewkesbury Abbey

Chapter Four

The children have been entertained for the weekend, and all the household chores taken care of, in readiness for our departure this morning. We are beginning this phase of the trip almost on our doorstep, with just six miles to travel to Bayham Abbey, which is set in a valley on the Kent/Sussex border. This is the only surviving Premonstratensian house in England which was directly dependent on the foundation's mother-house in Premontre, France. (The other abbey was St Radegund's, not far from the Kent coast between Dover and Folkestone, where all that survives are a few crumbled mounds of flint, and fragments of remaining walls incorporated in a farmhouse, and a deteriorating gatehouse.)

Bayham has a wonderfully tranquil and romantic aura, and it is very easy to understand why it is such a popular situation for wedding ceremonies, as we have witnessed on two earlier visits. From the early 14th Century façade of the Kentish gate, beside the river, it is possible to view the extent of these remarkable ruins on this neatly lawned site. Standing in the 'new' crossing, with its superb clustered columns forming the pier of the north transept, it is difficult to understand why such an extravagant re-modelling of the church took place after less than a hundred years. As we proceed to the east end of the church, the space vacated by the east window is now filled with a majestic old beech tree, its knotted, tangle of roots gripping the surviving wall like elderly, arthritic fingers. Somehow this portrays such a sense of strength and vigour, almost breathing eternal life into these ancient, hallowed stones. Apart from the church, the chapterhouse and the sparse remains of the monks' dormitory and living quarters, no other buildings have been excavated. In fact, quite the reverse. During the 18th Century, when the site was landscaped to provide a 'romantic ruin' backdrop to the newly-built manor house, some parts were deliberately buried to enhance the garden aspect.

Having visited the abbey countless times in the past, purely for recreational purposes, we had a reasonably good idea of its layout and features. We were, therefore, quite surprised at how much of the architectural detail, skilfully worked in the gorgeous yellow sandstone, we had overlooked previously. During the last nine weeks our eyes had obviously become accustomed to focusing on the finer points of detail which, in the past, went almost unnoticed. It is time to leave the peaceful ruins of Bayham Abbey for today, but their ease of accessibility from home ensures that many more peaceful hours may be spent there in the future.

Travelling down towards the Sussex coast, we drive through the busy High Street in Battle, until we see the formidable medieval gatehouse of Battle Abbey, dominating the marketplace. The 'Swift' is easily parked in the large, tree-lined car park at the western edge of this famous, historical site. Although the grounds are quite extensive, very little remains of the Benedictine monastery, founded by William the Conqueror in honour of his victory at the Battle of Hastings. Nothing of the church or the main claustral buildings survive, but the vast, roofless dormitory with a magnificent vaulted undercroft providing three sizeable day rooms, can be seen in much of their former glory. The tallest room at the southern end is believed to have been the novices' room, and the room at the far end was possibly the monks' common room. Looking over to the western edge of the cloister, the original wall of the Abbot's Hall (now forming part of Battle Abbey School), still retains traces of the magnificent vaulting that once formed the covered walkway around the cloister. Other features of the site include a plaque indicating where King Harold fell (at the position of the original high altar) an amazingly excavated crypt beneath the east end chevet of the church which still has a beautiful piscina set in one of the chapels, and, of course, the infamous battlefield.

In three and a half hours, we had completed our work schedule for today and were now driving into Bexhill to pick up a delicious fish 'n' chip lunch before going to see my parents for the afternoon. With travelling around for the last ten weeks, we'd been unable to do the family rounds, so we are taking the opportunity today whilst in the area. The added bonus is that we get to sleep 'indoors' tonight.

Even with the space, and warmth, of 'en suite' facilities and the luxury of having breakfast prepared for us, it didn't compensate for the miserable, wet and windy morning we had awoken to. This is the south coast, and the middle of June, for goodness sake — I think somebody has re-written the script!

Our drive to Boxgrove seemed exceptionally slow and difficult with the prevailing weather conditions, and we sincerely hoped that we were not going to finish our tour in the same vein as we had begun it. On the road out of the village, we noticed the sign for Boxgrove Priory and, on the opposite side of the road, a public car park. Raincoats and camera equipment collected, we walked down the lane to the remains of this Benedictine priory, the quire of which survived as the parish church. The huge stone columns and austere rounded arches of the Norman nave, happily reside with the clustered shafts in Purbeck marble and the graceful pointed arches built at a later stage. There are traces of a beautiful wall painting, and the remains of some Norman fresco painting, as well as a superb example of a piscina from the original priory. Laurie was disappointed that photographic opportunities were non-existent because the church was in the process of being transformed into a theatre, with stage, bench seating, and spotlights being erected everywhere. Apparently we'd arrived on the opening day of Boxgrove's Classical Concerts Week and we were advised that if we stood still for too long we'd be commandeered into helping with the preparations!

Bayham Abbey — **Kent**
The beech tree's tangled roots emerging from the high altar

Making a fairly swift exit, we decided to explore the ruinous fragments of the old priory and guest house in the grounds surrounding the church. Photographically, the scene was even less promising, with an enormous marquee almost obliterating the remains of the chapterhouse, several workmen carrying out repair work to the footings of the old nave, and the 'stage builders' rushing to and fro with large sections of boarding. Although it appears to be a charming site, the full atmospheric beauty of Boxgrove has been lost amidst the sheer volume of bodies and activity. We will return!

A couple of miles further along the A27 and we are in Chichester. Maybe this will be 'third time lucky' for us to research the interior of the cathedral, our two previous visits having to be aborted by circumstances beyond our control. At least it's stopped raining so the walk from the car park is quite pleasant, and it enables Laurie to spend some time photographing the external aspects of this magnificent 12th Century cathedral, before venturing inside.

Finally managing to see the inside of Chichester Cathedral, I found my initial reaction to this cold, bland space a little disappointing. There were a couple of elaborate stone carved panels in the South Aisle, fragments of a 2nd Century Roman mosaic floor below, and some beautiful 16th Century paintings on wooden panels in the transepts. Otherwise, much of the artwork and general décor was very modern and did not particularly appeal to me, but I am sure the skilful work is appreciated by the less narrow-minded visitors. What I did particularly like to see were the numbers of elderly people being encouraged to 'lunch out' in the cathedral, with the prospect of a concert to entertain them while they were tucking in to their tea and sandwiches. Talking of lunch, it's about time we left Chichester and drove on to Selsey.

Catching up with Laurie's grandmother is our next priority, as we are only some fifteen miles from Selsey and have the rest of the afternoon free to visit her. Ensuring that we'd had sufficient tea and cake, she waved us on our way just after five o'clock, when we went in search of our CL for the night, listed as being on the edge of a bird sanctuary. Strange — all I noticed were greenhouses, old cars and some kind of market garden nursery.

Today looked like being a blustery 'sunshine and showers' day, traditionally the kind of weather expected in April. Nevertheless, it was dry as we drove the thirty miles to our first destination in Hampshire and, if we were quick, we could manage to dodge the large black cloud that was slowly drifting towards us. Parking the motorhome in the spacious nursery car park, we walked back down to the main road to find the entrance to Titchfield Abbey. The gate was padlocked, and there wasn't a soul in sight. I walked back to the nursery to enquire if there was a warden for the site, but meanwhile Laurie had called at the pub opposite to find the landlady held a key, and an information leaflet on the history of Tichfield Abbey.

Battle Abbey — *East Sussex*
A delightful surviving piscina in the crypt,
amongst the spreading confusion of wild flowers

Bayham Abbey — *Kent*
An elaborate corbel

The nave of this 13th Century Premonstratensian monastery had been converted to a grand, Elizabethan manor house for the 1st Earl of Southampton shortly after the Dissolution, and there is very little evidence of monastic construction or influence existing. Even the ruinous mansion looks sad and forlorn as it stands alone in an overgrown wilderness, enclosed by a high wall that virtually cuts it off from nearby civilisation. From all this destruction and decay, imagine my delight when I came across several small patches of medieval floor tiles that would have adorned the original abbey church. Laurie noticed a slim, decorative piece of column to photograph as it protruded from the brickwork of the conversion, which would probably have been part of the original chapterhouse.

That dark, threatening cloud is now looming overhead as we hurried back to the 'Swift', to begin our next leg of the journey to Netley Abbey. Two miles along the road and we're driving through a heavy downpour, but it does look brighter and clearer in the distance. Pulling into the car park at Netley, the rain has eased and is little more than a drizzle, so I put lunch in the oven, and then we set out to explore the extensive remains of this beautiful Cistercian abbey. There's a wonderful feeling of peace and serenity throughout the wooded valley where Netley lies, almost backing onto Southampton Water, even more noticeable today in the eerie, damp stillness of this showery weather. There is an abundance of finely carved detail, graceful lancet windows and intricate vaulted ceilings that have survived amazingly well over the last seven hundred years. From what is visible today, it surely must have been a grand, ornate monastery despite several financial difficulties during its construction. Following the Dissolution, it was common practice to convert these magnificent ecclesiastical buildings to luxurious mansions, and Netley suffered the same fate, with a huge Tudor manor house being born out of the nave and domestic buildings of the abbey.

During the early 18th Century, the great abbey church was nearly lost forever when it was sold for building materials. However, as the builder began to demolish the west end, some window tracery fell onto him and killed him, and this was taken as a 'sign' from on high not to proceed with the work. So one man's misadventure was instrumental in preserving these superb ruins for the enjoyment of many more generations. Your death was not in vain, sir.

On the far side of the site, in the abbot's lodgings, we took shelter from a sudden cloudburst and looked across to the claustral buildings given a fresh, new sheen with the torrential rain pounding against the ancient stonework. Laurie insisted on staying for a while to capture the rain-washed beauty of certain features on the site, but I made a hasty dash back to the motorhome to put the finishing touches to lunch.

We've dried out, eaten lunch and had a cup of tea, and now felt refreshed

Battle Abbey — *East Sussex*
The impressive vaulted undercroft of the day room

Tichfield Abbey — *Hampshire*
One of many small sections of medieval floor tiles

Tichfield Abbey — *Hampshire*
The nave after its Elizabethan conversion

and ready to continue our journey to Romsey. Our previous visit to Romsey Abbey had been necessarily brief, but today we intended to make a thorough investigation of this wonderful Norman abbey, built on the site of a Saxon nunnery. The massive round pillars, with elaborately decorated arches three storeys high, are sheer Norman simplicity and style. Medieval floor tiles in excellent condition, showing the Crusades, are laid in front of the altar in one of the chapels, and in another of the chapels is a superb 12th Century wall painting. My overall impression of Romsey is one of awe and wonderment that this ancient house of worship seems almost untouched by time, and is a rare example of how much skilled craftsmanship was employed in the construction of these enormous abbeys.

Back outside the heavy showers appear to be overshadowing the sunny intervals and we decide not to follow our former plan of re-visiting Mottisfont Abbey and Gardens, just four miles outside of Romsey. Our trip there last year was on a very warm spring afternoon where we enjoyed strolling through the beautiful grounds beside the River Test, as well as discovering the remaining evidence of the 12th Century Augustinian priory. We felt it would not have quite the same appeal in today's unpredictable conditions, taking afternoon tea in the old tennis courts surrounded by the rose garden! Nonetheless, it is a delightful site, maintained by The National Trust, and well worth a visit.

Of course, the other determining factor in our movements today is the commencement of the World Cup, and we need to find our camp site and prepare for the opening match — so I'm reliably informed! The club site was three miles outside of Winchester, on fairly high ground, and should enable us to receive a good signal for TV reception.

It continued to rain hard throughout the evening and well into the night. Laurie was suffering with recurring 'bad memories' syndrome, and dreamt of tow ropes, tractors and deep boggy pitches, parked, as we were, on a grass pitch some distance from the gravel roadway of the site!

His panic was totally unfounded — the site was well-drained, with a good gravel base — and we drove effortlessly off the site this morning, arriving in the city of Winchester by 8.30. Having had to get up early for years, whilst commuting to London, our body clocks had become pre-programmed and we actually found it very difficult to 'sleep in'. Although sometimes it meant that we arrived at a site before it opened, when we were travelling into the cities, it did have the major advantage of allowing us to park with a certain degree of ease.

From a photographic point of view, our visit to Winchester Cathedral was a complete 'non-starter'. There was scaffolding and workmen everywhere, inside and out, due to an extensive programme of restoration work being

Chichester Cathedral — *West Sussex*
The medieval cloisters

Netley Abbey — *Hampshire*
South transept and chapterhouse from the cloister garth

carried out. We very quickly resigned ourselves to the fact that we would have to defer our research work on this cathedral until a later date.

Suddenly gaining an extra couple of hours in the itinerary, I wondered if I might be able to trace a former work colleague, whom I understood had moved to Winchester about a year ago. After consulting the local telephone directories, the library, the council and other 'hunches', I surrendered to the challenge, and went to take a look at the Great Hall and the old castle foundations instead. The main attraction for me, with my fascination for Arthurian legend (in common, as I understand, with Henry III), was the superb replica of King Arthur's Round Table, proudly displayed on the wall of the Great Hall.

We then walked out of the city and past Winchester College to find Wolvesey, sometimes referred to as a castle but was, in fact, the old Bishops' Palace. Although an extensive site (some eight acres), very little of the Norman palace has survived but perhaps just sufficient for us to imagine what a huge and impressive building this must have been. Winchester was the wealthiest diocese in the Middle Ages and, therefore, the bishops held the highest and most important offices in the church, and they lived in this once magnificent palace. It is known that some sort of structure has been in existence on the site of 'Wulf's island' for over one thousand years, and a continuous building programme to improve and enlarge the palace was carried out during three centuries. The English Heritage guidebook gives a very detailed account of the fascinating history of Wolvesey.

Another interesting historical connection with Winchester, was the founding of The Hospital of St Cross, a few miles from the city centre. Henry de Blois, Bishop of Winchester in the early 1100s, was responsible for this charitable institution run by the Cluniac monks to help the starving families of that time. The site comprises the brothers' living accommodation — there are twenty-five lay brothers still in residence — a beautiful Norman church, a 14th Century kitchen and hall, and the garden. It is an extremely peaceful and thought-provoking place, with a history that belies the sedate and orderly environment the residents enjoy today.

With the weather remaining wet and dismal, we consider driving on to Salisbury Cathedral this afternoon — at least part of our work could be completed under cover! Walking back to where we had parked the motorhome, we noticed a prominent 'Eldridge Pope' sign on the opposite side of the road about 300 yards further along. Laurie then proceeded to enlighten me with the relevant facts of this particular brewery and its production of a favourite beer that he had not been able to buy in Kent. Needless to say, we took the short detour to arrive at the off licence and duly purchased a few bottles of said ale for his future consumption.

Romsey Abbey — *Hampshire*
Beautiful 13th Century painted wooden panel

Netley Abbey — *Hampshire*
Looking through an elaborate doorway from the cloister garth

Romsey Abbey — *Hampshire*
A rare example of a complete Norman nunnery

Back in the 'Swift', we switched on the mobile phone to be confronted with a panic-stricken message from our 'housesitter'. Apparently she'd locked herself out of the house, called a locksmith to her assistance — who'd proceeded to ruin the lock and still leave her stranded on the outside of the house — and was now in need of further suggestions for gaining entry! With over 200 miles separating us, a work schedule to complete, and miserable weather and road conditions to contend with, we were not really in the frame of mind to want to deal with this inconvenient matter. However, following a series of phone calls, some semblance of a solution was reached, the housesitter had calmed down, and we ate a quick lunch 'on the road' and continued our journey to Salisbury.

Yet further frustration and disappointment as we got our first view of the cathedral; over half the external walls were completely obliterated with scaffolding. Inside, Salisbury Cathedral was heaving with parties of French and American tourists being led around by their very loud-speaking guides. I was more than happy just to find a quiet corner where I could sit and read the guidebook, while Laurie battled with the human element to photograph the main features and vistas of this vast and elegant church. Although built over 700 years ago, its superior haughtiness felt strangely ageless and cold.

Towards the end of the afternoon, the weather actually began to brighten a little and so we thought it would be fitting to visit Old Sarum, the site of the ancient city of Salisbury. High on this exposed hilltop, people settled here over five thousand years ago, and there is much evidence to suggest that it was an important centre in Roman times. However, it really began to flourish in the early part of the 11th Century when the Normans commenced building the castle, a cathedral and a royal palace. All that can be seen today are the massive earthworks, a few low sections of castle wall and a plan of the cathedral marked out in the grass. But the evocative atmosphere among these demolished and abandoned ruins can conjure up stirring visions of life covering such a vast period of history that it leaves you feeling quite stunned.

I think I've OD'd on history and religion today and tiredness has now set in with a vengeance. The drive back to the caravan site at Winchester seemed endless, but once we'd pitched for the night, dinner was quickly prepared, and accompanied by a bottle of Eldridge Pope Royal Oak beer. It was indeed a fine ale!

I am not sure whether it was the strong beer, the constant battering from the tiresome weather yesterday, or simply trying to cram so many visits into a single day, but I remember very little of the night. Totally refreshed, and enthused by the early signs of sunshine, blue sky and fluffy white clouds, we leave Winchester and travel west into Dorset. Approximately fifty miles along the A30 and we arrive in Shaftesbury, to make our second visit to the delightful garden site of the original Benedictine nunnery founded in the late

Salisbury Cathedral — *Wiltshire*
The tower as seen through a cinqfoil in the cloisters

Shaftesbury Abbey — *Dorset*
A profusion of daisies bursts forth in this peaceful garden that
once housed an important abbey with strong royal connections

9th Century by King Alfred for his daughter. We parked the 'Swift' in the small, town car park and weaved our way through the narrow streets to Park Walk where we entered the newly re-furbished shop, and museum.

Today was a perfect day to fully appreciate the colourful splendour and the pleasant fragrances of this peaceful garden, which included several clusters of magnificent blood-red poppies contrasting with masses of snowy-white Michaelmas daisies. Considering the importance of Shaftesbury Abbey during its lifetime, and its strong royal connections, it is astonishing that the church has been reduced to no more than a few piles of rubble, just visible beneath the profusion of wild flowers. Apart from a small 13th Century crypt, uncovered during excavations over the last 150 years, no substantial structure exists, but there are some good examples of carved stonework and medieval floor tiles on display in the museum. Talking to the curator at the site, she informed us that further excavation work was to be carried out this year and was hopeful that much more of the abbey church would be discovered. Whatever the excavations uncover, I am sure nothing could enhance the blissful tranquillity and beauty of this ruinous nunnery — it is just a pure and simple delight.

Travelling further down the A30, we are stopping to visit Sherborne Abbey, which began life as a Saxon cathedral, then became a Benedictine monastery, and today is used as the parish church. A far cry from the fate of Shaftesbury, just twenty minutes away. Laurie was, once again, in his element as Sherborne Abbey is an ideal photographic subject, built of warm, golden stone that almost shimmers in the sunlight. Inside the church, there are so many architectural styles to feast upon which clearly depict all three periods of use. There is the most exquisite fan-vaulting throughout the abbey which has, quite remarkably, survived for over 500 years. An incredible feeling of warmth and protection radiates from the ancient stonework, as well as a great sense of peace and sanctity. It is a marvellous building with a fascinating history and a wealth of treasures to discover. We eventually leave the abbey and walk back towards the town, passing under the bow arch (currently tumbling with pretty mauve aubretia), and arriving at the lavatorium. The day had become extremely warm and sunny, so what better way to enjoy an hour's break than sitting outside the 'oldy worldy' pub opposite, with a pint of 'Royal Oak', watching the townsfolk scurrying about their business. A great welcome back to the 20th Century!

Another 'car park' lunch was eaten back at the 'Swift' before we drove the mile to Sherborne Old Castle. Our intention was to seek out a sunny, sheltered corner against the ruinous walls and catch up on some reading and writing. But, as with all the best-laid plans, the sun swiftly disappeared behind the ever-increasing cloud and the blustery wind had a chilly edge as it swept across the exposed castle site. Back to the motorhome, and plan B!

Although cloudy, the weather remained dry and, as it was only 3.30 p.m., we looked through our guidebooks for somewhere less exposed to spend another hour or so before going on to the camp site, at Wincanton Racecourse. The National Trust provided an ideal spot to unwind and take a leisurely stroll around the lake and gardens, at Stourhead.

When we arrived at the racecourse, the ground·looked quite boggy, and the darkening sky overhead was threatening more rain in the not too distant future. The site wardens permitted us to park on the roadway, in front of the grandstand, which kept Laurie reasonably happy in the knowledge that whatever Mother Nature 'threw' at us during the night, we would be able to make a clean departure the next morning!

Following an unusually disturbed night, it was 10.15 a.m. before we awoke on Saturday morning, but as we had no definite plans for the day — and the weather was atrocious — we continued with the morning routine in unhurried fashion. Originally, we had scheduled a visit to Bath Abbey but had since decided that on a busy Saturday morning, this was probably not the ideal opportunity to take good, library photos, or contend with the volume of weekend traffic.

Eventually we drove up to Berkeley Castle, situated just off the M5 in the Vale of Berkeley. As the heavy rain continued, we made a quick dash to the castle entrance and sought a temporary respite from the wet and dreary conditions with a tour of the internal rooms of this vast family home. It appears that some sort of structure, perhaps quite primitive, has been in existence on this site since the mid-11th Century, and has remained in the same family throughout its life. The house and history are fascinating, with its main 'claim to fame' being the place where Edward II was gruesomely murdered. Outside, the grounds are beautifully kept and the recent rainfall had accentuated the freshness and colour of the plants and flowers. From the lawn as we looked up at this rugged, old fortress built of stone displaying the most amazing hues of pinks and mauves, it was easy to imagine how this solid mass had survived over 850 years.

Having eaten a late lunch 'a la car park', we ventured out again to take a quick walk around the Butterfly Farm — another of my fascinations. Emerging from the humidity of the exotic bufferflies' tropical paradise, we made our final damp trek across the car park back to the motorhome. After a cup of tea, and a change of clothes, we left Berkeley and drove to Cirencester to book into the caravan club site we'd used on our previous visit to Gloucestershire. A quiet night in tonight, with a nice meal, a bottle of wine and the England World Cup football match!

Sunday dawned bright and warm and we took an early-morning stroll into the

Shaftesbury Abbey — **Dorset**
Fragments almost hidden by a bold display of blood-red poppies

ancient town of Cirencester, a thriving and important centre during Roman times. It was blissfully free from cars and people, the only sounds being the distant peel of the resonant church bells beckoning the Sunday worshippers to rise from their beds and present themselves for morning service.

Two hours, a cup of coffee, and a huge sticky bun, later we set off to complete this phase of the tour with a research trip to Gloucester Cathedral. Parked conveniently in front of the west precinct wall of the old Benedictine monastery, we walk through the 12th Century gateway and behold this magnificently ornate, pale-yellow sandstone church. As seems to be the norm, we are also confronted with a maze of scaffold poles and boards, which rather restricts Laurie's creativity with the camera yet again. Even inside, the scaffolding was creeping up the walls between the enormous Norman nave columns, which prevented many 'angles' from being satisfactorily photographed. Nevertheless, we gathered sufficient material for our initial research and would return at a future date for a more detailed inspection of its features.

On our way back to the motorhome, we walked past the little cloister and the remaining arches of the monastic infirmary, a gentle reminder of the monks' care and companionship for each other throughout their lives.

With time to cram in just one more visit on the final day of our historical adventures across Great Britain, we head for Sudeley Castle, just northeast of Cheltenham, in the Cotswolds. This is a charming mixture of restored family manor house, and romantic ruinous outbuildings (including a lovely chapel), all encompassed within delightfully landscaped gardens. Throughout its colourful history, Sudeley has suffered great destruction at the hands of Cromwell, and been financially crippled through death duties and the two World Wars. It is, therefore, all the more amazing to see what has been achieved by the present owners, who have transformed Sudeley Castle into a prosperous and rewarding business venture, without detracting from its importance as a superb historic monument and, overall, a comfortable family residence.

That's it — all done! Back to Circencester for our last night in the confined comforts of the 'Swift', and relieved at the achievement of our initial plan, despite all early concerns, fears and frustrations. I can scarcely believe that we have spent a quarter of this year travelling, working, and living in this cosy mobile space, which now feels more like home than the house we have lived in for only four months. In many ways, I have mixed feelings about returning to a state of normality — sadness at the loss of adventure, a contentedness to settle back into our new house, and elation at the prospect of beginning the next phase of the grand plan, the manuscript! It was an exhilarating, educational and enthralling experience, and one I shall enjoy relating to my grandchildren in years to come (before they are old enough to

Sherborne Abbey — ***Dorset***
Exqusite fan vaulting on the presbytery ceiling

Sherborne Abbey — ***Dorset***
A 'chocolate box' view of this wonderful old abbey church

Gloucester Cathedral
The richly painted ceiling in one of the small chapels

read the book!).

Last night sleep did not come easy, and this morning I am in a state of lethargy and anticlimax. The day looks dull and overcast (which matches my mood perfectly), and rain is forecast. Well, at least some things have remained consistent until the end, and the inclement weather has, unfortunately, been one of the more reliable factors of the trip. Having completed a mini-overhaul of all services 'on board', we point the 'Swift' in the direction of home, via a network of motorways, and a brief stopover at Laurie's parents.

Back in Kent, and we decide this work would not be complete without a return visit to one of the few priories that has re-established itself and is still inhabited by a community of Benedictine nuns. Close to the Kent coast, on the former Isle of Thanet, is the site of one of the first nunneries in England, dating back to AD670. However, the abbey ruins and cloisters that survive are of a much later Norman restoration, although the oldest wing of the priory still in use, is Saxon, and dates from the early 11th Century. Throughout the last 1300 years, Minster Abbey has indeed experienced a chequered history, having suffered destruction twice, demolition (following the Dissolution) of chapel and outbuildings, and restoration to a Tudor manor house. In 1928 Mr Senior, the current owner then, had excavations made and ancient foundations (and the site of St Mildred's 8th Century tomb) were uncovered.

Then in 1937 a small group of Bavarian nuns returned to Minster and set up their community in the old house. Following the Second World War, and occupation by The Royal Artillery, the present community finally returned to the abbey in 1945. Our trip was made even more memorable by the mother prioress, whose Scottish, forthright manner, genteel charm, and vast historical knowledge, brought this old priory back to life for us. Unfortunately, she informed us of her pending 'retirement' so although you may not be treated to her sense of humour and love of life at Minster, you will always be able to experience the serenity of this small, but important, historical monument.

It is a Saturday, it is getting late and the traffic is horrendous (as usual, in this part of the country), so you will have to excuse the obvious omission of Canterbury Cathedral and St Augustine's Abbey, just twelve miles away from Minster. However, we did travel a couple of miles further along the road to visit the site of St Augustine's Cross. This 19th Century stone monument is a replica of the Celtic cross that marked the landing site of St Augustine in 597, before he went on to found the abbey in the same year. Being 'local' we have visited the abbey ruins and the cathedral on many previous occasions — and will do so again in the not too distant future — but for now we will simply tease the tastebuds by saying that this is where Christianity was first established in the Anglo-Saxon realms, and it is a fascinating trail to discover 'what happened next!'.

Minster Abbey — *Kent*

The small dark stained-glass window by the entrance to the crypt

St Augustine's Cross — *Kent*

A 19th Century replica of the Celtic cross commemorating the saint's arrival in England to spread the word of Christianity

You may be even more amazed, or astounded, that possibly the most famous of all abbeys has been excluded from this tour. This was deliberate. After twelve weeks freedom from the general bustle, hassle and polluted environment of our capital City, there was not even the slightest chance that we were going back to explore the renowned beauty and breath-taking delights of Westminster Abbey. We will quite happily leave these for you to investigate at your leisure.

Minster Abbey — *Kent*
The bare and simple crypt of this early Norman abbey has survived

Epilogue

We've been home a week already, had the 1800 slides developed from Laurie's photographic efforts, held several discussions on the proposed manuscript, and set up our own company. Time doesn't stand still, as they say, and before our ideas become as eroded as most of the sites we visited, we need to commit them to print. I realise this is really where the hard work begins, and the last three months will soon seem like a holiday compared to the task that lies ahead of us. Moreover, most of the time I will be assembling the text and data in the quiet solitude of my recently-converted conservatory-cum-office disturbed only by the constant humming of all the hi-tech equipment surrounding me.

Laurie also has to re-adjust to commuting back to 'the smoke' every day and having the restrictions of suits, offices, timetables and 'power lords' thrust upon him once again! Naturally, this is only a temporary arrangement until such time as we can accumulate sufficient funds to plan another trip through the intrepid scenes of our history.

Taking everything into consideration, however, I would not have missed the experience (even the not-so-good bits!) for anything. Having spent a total of sixty-one days 'on the road', covering some 6,735 miles throughout England, Wales and parts of Scotland, seen so many inspiring sights, and greatly improved my knowledge of history, geography (and orienteering), it will be something to remember for a long time to come. Nobody can take that away from us. Everyone can have their steady, well paid City jobs, with the inevitable aggravations and boring routines that accompany those positions, but now I've tasted the freedom and adventure of the open road, I want more! Soon.

Watercolour of the picturesque remains of Valle Crucis Abbey

GLOSSARY

ABBEY	*A monastic house ruled by an abbot or abbess*
AMBULATORY	*A place for walking, often covered*
APSE	*A semicircular or polygonal east end of church or chapel*
ARCADING	*Decoration in the form of a series of arches*
AUGUSTINIAN	*Followers of St Augustine of Hippo, leading lives of poverty, celibacy and obedience*
BENEDICTINE	*First formal monastic rule that formed the basis for all early Christian monastic activity*
BLIND ARCADING	*Closed with masonry, often used as decorative wall strengthening*
BOSS	*Carved and decorated ornaments set at the intersection of rib and vaulting*
CAPITOL	*The crowning head of a column or pier giving support to arches or vaulting ribs*
CARTHUSIAN	*A contemplative order of monks, bound to silence, and who lived as virtual hermits*
CATHEDRAL	*A church containing the bishop's seat*
CHAPTERHOUSE	*A building employed for meetings of a cathedral or monastic chapter*
CHEVET	*Radiating chapels and ambulatory of an apsidal east end*
CISTERCIAN	*An order of white monks who followed a brand of Benedictinism of extreme strictness*
CLAUSTRAL	*Associated with, or belonging to, a cloister*
CLOISTER	*A four-sided enclosure with a covered walkway or alley along each side*
CLUNIAC	*Named after the monastery at Cluny, founded in 910, the order following strict Benedictinism and devoted to personal spirituality and concern for ceremony*
COMMENDATOR	*A lay abbot (Scotland)*
CORBEL	*A stone or wooden projection from a wall, often used as a support*
CRYPT	*A vaulted chamber beneath the church*
DAY STAIRS	*Access from the dorter to the cloister*
DECORATED	*Architectural period (Gothic) 1307-1377*
DIOCESE	*Ecclesiastical territory governed by a bishop*
DISSOLUTION	*A process of closure of the monasteries by Henry VIII from 1536 to 1540*
DORTER	*The monks' dormitory*
EARLY ENGLISH	*The first English (Gothic) architectural style following the Norman period*
FRATER/REFECTORY	*The monks' dining room*
GOTHIC	*Architectural style from 12th — 15th Century using pointed arches*
INFIRMARY	*A building where the sick and aged within a monastic community were cared for*
JACOBEAN	*Architectural style during the Stuart period (17th Century)*
LADY CHAPEL	*Dedicated to the Blessed Virgin Mary, and normally built to the east of the high altar*

LANCET	*A high, narrow window with a pointed head*
LATRINE	*Gutter or drainage channel*
LAVATORIUM	*A trough in the cloister where the monks could wash their hands before meals*
LAY BROTHERS	*Monks not in holy orders who performed manual labour*
MANSIO	*Official guesthouse for travelling Roman civil servants*
MINSTER	*Originally meaning any monastery, monastic establishment or its church*
NAVE	*Main body of church extending in a west-east direction*
NIGHT STAIRS	*Access from the dorter to the church*
NORMAN	*The English variant of Romanesque style during 11th & 12th Centuries before Gothic*
PERPENDICULAR	*Architectural period 1377-1485*
PILGRIMAGE OF GRACE	*A movement of the common people, whose leadership was taken over by lawyers, gentry and noblemen, and whose purpose was the protestation against high prices, the ill-effects of land enclosures, the introduction of the Bible in English, and the conduct and policies of Henry VIII's chief civil servants*
PISCINA	*A small basin in a wall niche close to an altar, used for washing sacramental vessels*
PREMONSTRATENSIAN	*Followers of the Order of St Norbet, founded at Premontre in 1120, adhering to the rule of St Augustine with additional austerities, e.g. abstinence from meat*
PRESBYTERY	*The eastern part of a church, containing the high altar*
PRIORY	*A religious house, frequently of lower standing than an abbey, and headed by a prior or prioress*
QUIRE/CHOIR	*Area of church, between nave and presbytery, where the stalls are situated, and where the monks sat to sing their offices. In modern times, it is usually where the clergy sit*
REREDORTER	*A building containing the latrines*
REREDOS	*An ornamental screen, curtain or wall behind the altar*
ROMANESQUE	*A building style between Roman times and the Gothic phase in the 12th Century*
SACRISTY	*A place that held the sacred vessels and vestments*
SAVIGNIAC	*Founded in 1105 at Savigny, originally as a colony of hermits, and later merged with the Cistercians*
SEDILIA	*Special, decorative seats either side of the altar for clergy and servers to sit*
SLYPE	*A covered way, or passage, usually leading to the cloister*
TIRONENSIAN	*Founded in 1117 at Tiron and influenced by the contemporary Cistercian rule*
TRACERY	*Pattern of open stonework in the upper section of a window or archway*
TRANSEPT	*Part of the church which crosses the nave in a north-south direction*
UNDERCROFT	*A crypt or vault below the floor of the church, or important apartment in a monastery*
VAULTING	*Roof spaces between columns and arches*